*Inside the Halo
and Beyond*

Also by Maxine Kumin

POETRY

Selected Poems 1960–1990
Connecting the Dots
Looking for Luck
Nurture
The Long Approach
Our Ground Time Here Will Be Brief
The Retrieval System
House, Bridge, Fountain, Gate
Up Country
The Nightmare Factory
The Privilege
Halfway

NOVELS

Quit Monks or Die!
The Designated Heir
The Abduction
The Passions of Uxport
Through Dooms of Love

SHORT STORIES

Why Can't We Live Together Like Civilized Human Beings?

ESSAYS

In Deep: Country Essays
To Make a Prairie: Essays on Poets, Poetry, and Country Living

ESSAYS AND STORIES

Women, Animals, and Vegetables

MAXINE KUMIN

Inside the Halo and Beyond

The Anatomy of a Recovery

W. W. NORTON & COMPANY
NEW YORK • LONDON

"Sonnet of Intimacy" by Vinicius de Moraes, from *Anthology of Twentieth Century Brazilian Poetry* © 1997, Wesleyan University Press by permission of the University Press of New England.

Copyright © 2000 by Maxine Kumin

For information about permission to reproduce selections from this book, write to Permissions, W. W. Norton & Company, Inc., 500 Fifth Avenue, New York, NY 10110

The text of this book is composed in Palatino
Book design and composition by Dana Sloan
Manufacturing by Quebecor Vermont

Library of Congress Cataloging-in-Publication Data

Kumin, Maxine, date.
Inside the halo and beyond : the anatomy of a recovery / Maxine Kumin.
p. cm.

1. Kumin, Maxine, date. 2. Spinal cord—Wounds and injuries—Patients—United States—Biography. 3. Poets, American—20th century—Biography. 4. Driving of horse-drawn vehicles. I. Title.

PS3521.U638 Z468 2000
,811'.54—dc21
[B]

ISBN: 978-0-393-32261-3   99-087262

W. W. Norton & Company, Inc.
500 Fifth Avenue, New York, N. Y. 10110
www.wwnorton.com

W. W. Norton & Company Ltd.
Castle House, 75/76 Wells Street, London W1T 3QT

1 2 3 4 5 6 7 8 9 0

For Kathy Waine
who saved my life
and
for Judith Kumin
who helped me reconstruct it

I

July 21, 1998

～　　A perfect midsummer day in Vermont, the world in full leaf, sunny but with a fair breeze. Ideal for the last driving clinic before the gala three-day carriage-driving show this coming weekend. About a dozen of us, including two pairs—carriages drawn by matched horses—are warming up on a large grassy area enclosed by a fence on one long side, buildings on another. A stone wall at the top of the field divides it from the state road. We're going to practice driving figures for the dressage phase of the show. Just as ice skaters have certain patterns they must execute in competition, carriage drivers also must demonstrate patterns including circles, serpentines, changes of direction and pace, good square halts, and backing up in straight lines.

There are two new horses here today; they look like young Arabians with their pretty little dished profiles. It's going to be a nuisance to integrate them into our already cohesive group. The owners put one in a stall and hitch the other to drive. The stabled horse whinnies frantically when his buddy leaves. Then he leaps up over the four-foot dutch door and races out onto the field, where we're all intently moving on our own, concentrating on getting our horses limber and balanced before the formal session with our driving instructor begins.

Although they've never met before, the loose horse makes a beeline for my horse Deuter, perhaps attracted by his bright red chestnut color, and runs into him head on. I feel Deuter jitter and suck back behind the bit. Is he going to rear and then plunge forward to escape?

"Easy, Dude," I tell him. " Eas-ay, eas-ay," words he knows but doesn't always honor.

Finally, one of the owners runs out with a lead shank and captures the little loose horse. Crisis past, Deuter seems to relax in my hands. He rounds over nicely on the bit, and comes across the diagonal at an extended trot, a little overeager but presumably none the worse for the encounter.

"Talk about déjà vu all over again," the instructor says as we come past her. "That was quite a flashback he had. Some things they never forget." She's a highly regarded woman in the horse world, not only as a trainer and driver but also for what I call horse charisma, her ability to "read" an animal from the way he is moving and responding.

I agree with her as we trot past. "He almost lost it there but I think he's over it," I say, and we cross the field once more out of her line of sight. The very first time we hitched him at this same facility, he was run into by a bridleless horse still attached to his cart. (Taking the bridle off before detaching the horse from the carriage is a breach of etiquette serious enough to get the miscreant disbarred.) Luckily, Deuter was safely out of the shafts at the time, but he fled in terror from the assault and ran two miles up a steep dirt road before the groom on a coach-and-four that was coming down the hill jumped off and retrieved him.

For at least a year Deuter became restive whenever another rig came toward him, particularly if the carriage was drawn by a pair of horses, with the attendant extra rattle and banging sounds. Now, though, he feels like his old self. My navigator, who has been riding on the back step of the carriage, dismounts and joins a group of observers on the sidelines.

Then, as we come to the top of the field along the stone wall, an immense piggyback logging truck roars up behind us, its multiple chains making a considerable racket.

Without warning, Deuter shifts out of his soft floating trot into a gallop. It takes me about three seconds to realize what he's done; I keep thinking he'll come back into my hands in another stride or two. We tear around one corner by the buildings and he bounces me out of my seat. I struggle to regain my balance and finally find the brake with my right foot, but even with all my weight on it, the mechanism is powerless to slow him down. There are all those carriages to steer around. I don't dare bail out. What if he runs into someone?

The carriage that I'm driving is a four-wheel metal marathon vehicle with a wedge seat that is supposed to hold the driver, or "whip, "securely in place. There's a stand on the rear for the navigator, or "groom," who accompanies the driver during the marathon phase of a driving show; the whole rig weighs about 350 pounds.

For the accident itself I have total amnesia. I come back to consciousness facedown, arms and legs asprawl. My limbs are numb, I am only vaguely aware they are still attached to me. Kathy, an old carriage-driving buddy who happens to be an emergency room nurse, is kneeling beside me, keeping me absolutely immobile. It is she who saves my life.

I gasp, "I can't breathe," and she comforts me. "Yes, you can. Just keep taking little sips of air."

Before the helicopter comes, before it swoops down beside me, the menacing roar of its rotors rousing me momentarily, I fade in and out of consciousness. Troughs and swells of pain suck me down, then spit me out. They roll me over and over, a pebble caught in this ocean where time has no limits and agony is without beginning or end. . . .

The helicopter lands on its tidy pad just outside the Trauma Center. I remember only fleeting moments of this experience—the terrible jolts of my stretcher being loaded and unloaded, the unspeakable, all-over pain. Victor, my husband, tells me they worked on me in the Trauma Center for about five hours while he sat in the waiting room. The doctors came and went every half hour with further news—of my punctured lung, of multiple broken ribs, of internal bleeding, and bruised kidney and liver, and loss of neurological function. "Oh my God, oh my God," was all he could say at each notification, this man who is seldom at a loss for words.

July 22

Imagine a bird cage big enough for a large squawking parrot. Nothing fancy; no rococo bars with curlicues at the top, just a sturdy cage fashioned from titanium and graphite, but missing a few bars front and back. Imagine a human head inside the cage fastened by four titanium pins that dig into the skull. The pins are as sharp as ice picks. I wake up in this cage, disoriented, desperate, sicker than I have ever been. No feeling in my arms or legs, but a vague sense that my head is entrapped forever. No movement left or right, up or down. I am a stationary parrot inside my strict cage.

Some orthopedic wag dubbed this form of axial traction a halo. First applied in 1959, it was attached to a rigid full-body cast and was used to immobilize paralyzed polio patients whose airways were in danger because they could not hold their heads upright. Later, its usage extended to postop patients with cervical spine injuries, tumor removals, and congenital spinal malformations. The early halos, weighing upwards of ten pounds, were made of metal, which was opaque to X ray and was not MRI or CT scan compatible. Modern halos are made of lightweight composites. The full-body cast has given way to an adjustable plastic vest and the metal uprights of the cage are made of anodized metals so that they don't "seize" during tightening. Knurled bars are designed to prevent slipping; the entire halo must remain structurally intact.

Ancient Hindu epics report that Lord Krishna corrected the hunchback of one of his devotees using a similar device. What it was attached to is not recorded. In the modern version, the one-piece plastic vest is cut low enough in front to accommodate a woman's breasts, and is solid in back except for an opening for the spinal column. The vest fastens securely at the waist with thumbscrew fasteners spaced two inches apart. The instructions that come with the synthetic sheepskin liner caution against ever removing it. (It is, however, removable and replaceable after a shower or a workout in the therapy pool, neither of which I am permitted.)

The halo pins are still being redesigned. The exposed ends are secured with locknuts, and a little wrench is attached to the lower part of the cage, presumably to undo it in emergencies. The places where the picks grind into the cranium are euphemistically called pin sites. They must be kept clean by swabbing them twice a day with hydrogen peroxide in a normal saline solution.

I read that the "broad-shouldered pointed pin" is giving way to "a broad-shoulder pin with a bullet-shaped point" to make better contact with the skull and ensure "more rigidity at pin-bone interface." I read with a certain horrified fascination that the pins must be placed over the thicker portions of the skull—it had never occurred to me that there were thicker and thinner portions—so that the skull itself is not punctured. It follows that the pressure of the pins has to be applied correctly to get maximum fixation without breaking through the cranium. When the correct position for the pins has been determined, it takes a team of two using a torque wrench to tighten the pins by half turns at a time on opposite sides until the proper pressures—six pounds of torque—are reached. (Torque wrenches are calibrated to a certain force which cannot be exceeded; one need not be a physicist measuring force times distance to arrive at the appropriate measurement.) The front pins are placed on the forehead; the rear ones below the equator of the skull, which I take to be the greatest circumference of the head in question.

There are a number of caveats when it comes to pin placement: if a pin impacts the temporalis muscle, the patient may not only be in pain, he/she may not be able to chew. A pin inserted at the temporal bone may penetrate the thin layer there. The supraorbital nerve and frontal sinus are to be avoided. There are also issues of pin migration, which may dislocate the halo crown itself, and pin-site infection, which could endanger the whole process of restraint. (I was either unconscious or very heavily drugged when my pins were inserted; I am grateful to learn about these pitfalls after the fact.)

Applying the vest involves logrolling the patient, with support, so that the back shell of the vest can be slipped into place, then laying the patient supine to fit the front vest. The uprights of the cage must be evenly spaced on either side of the patient's head, the lateral bars connected to the uprights and to the halo and all bolts tightened to the proper torque—thirty feet/pounds for an adult. Fitting a child is dicier, as the young skull is thinner and may require more pins at a lower torque.

The medical articles that I have scanned stress how important it is to maintain communication between patient and physician. The patient should be informed of possible side effects and signs of problems. In my case, there was no such communication. I am glad I did not know that if a loose pin required more than two turns of the wrench to tighten, a new pin should be inserted in an adjacent site and the old pin removed. Nor was I aware that patients with foreheads that slope at a strong angle and patients with highly developed shoulder muscles, such as weight lifters, may require an extra pin behind each ear. Neither of these applied to me. I was uncomfortably familiar with pressure sores developing under the vest, with contact dermatitis and sweat rashes, and, most of all, with muscle tightness when lying down, for which the palliative of a small towel used as a neck roll provided little relief.

I am also glad I did not know that the halo does not totally inhibit motion of the vertebrae and that the most motion occurs when the patient goes from supine to upright or vice versa. In one study the overall motion measured was almost one third of normal range of motion; nevertheless, healing under this condition can take place.

Thousands of people are confined in halo restraints in the United States and Europe every year. At least ten companies are manufacturing these devices in the U.S. alone. Gradually I meet others of my kind, doggedly slogging around under the burden of our equipment, some tipped slightly forward, some tipped slightly back, to compensate for the neck fractures that landed us in this predicament in the first place.

I don't remember, or choose to remember, much about how I got here. It was Kathy who stabilized my head for almost an hour as I lay paralyzed on the field, Kathy who sent someone to call the rescue squad and who lobbied, once they arrived, for them to call in the Medivac team. Getting a helicopter takes protocol in this rural area, but once it was on the ground beside me, only six or eight minutes elapsed before I was airlifted to a local major medical center. I remember coming to and begging for painkillers en route, which the team is not permitted to administer. I remember kind strangers calling me "honey" and "sweetheart" and how this intimacy surprised me. I did not know then that they were afraid I would not survive the trip.

The vertebrae I broke are at the very top of the spinal column: C1, which is ring-shaped and fits around the odontoid, C2, which looks rather like a thumb. In the trade, one form of C2 break is known as the hangman's fracture, because the same vertebra is snapped when the trapdoor opens under the gallows. Mine, I learn long after the fact, is a Type II fracture, located in the narrowest region of the odontoid, the "waist" of the thumb.

Things are coming back to me little by little, but I am stuffing them down in a dirty laundry bag to be reviewed and shaken out later, when I get my courage back. I realize from the outset, though, that I've lost all

feeling in all four limbs, and I think at that moment I'd
rather be dead. In fact, thinking about being dead absorbs
a lot of my energy these first days. While I am pinioned
flat on my back, I am almost as black and blue with
grief and guilt for causing anguish to my family as is
my torn body. I have two black eyes and a large contu-
sion on my right cheekbone. My whole right side is
purple, shoulder and arm especially brilliant. Apparently
I have also punctured a lung, broken eleven ribs, bruised
a kidney and my liver, and suffered considerable internal bleeding. I've been given two units of packed red
blood cells. There's an IV line in the vein below my right
shoulder supplying me with morphine and glucose and
an oxygen tank feeds the tubes in my nostrils. These
accompany me as I am wheeled from CT scan to angi-
ogram to MRI.

(Later, I learn from my medical records, which I
devour with hungry voyeurism, that I occasionally came
to and spoke clearly while the paramedics applied a cervical spine board and turned me over, like an immense
beetle specimen, for transport. From my husband Victor's
E-mails to family and friends, I further learn how many
people were pulling for me from the outset. His com-
muniqués are detailed and invariably upbeat, even in
the first worst days: "Max's eye blink responses have

indicated alertness and she has begun to whisper-talk with the breathing tube out. Breathing gets better by the hour. Hematomas are receding. She's a REAL fighter which is of course why I wanted to marry her!")

I plead guilty to being a jock. I've been a jock all my life, from my adolescent days working out in the Broadmoor Pool in Philadelphia racing freestyle for the Women's Athletic Association, to my lengthy stint as a water safety instructor at summer camp. Horses, which had always been my passion, came back into my life when my daughter Judith was nine and caught the fever. It didn't take long to infect Victor as well. By then we had moved to the New Hampshire farm and were immersed in livestock. For more than a decade Victor and I travelled together as competitive trail riders on horses we had bred and midwifed and cared for, logging literally thousands of miles to condition our horses for the long rides.

Competitive trail rides and/or drives, over distances that range from twenty-five to one hundred miles, typically involve forty to fifty horses departing at one-minute intervals to complete a prescribed course within an ideal time. This is not a race. Every equine starts with a perfect score of 100. Points are deducted for fatigue, virtually imperceptible lamenesses, and pulse and respiration in excess of the parameters for that day, which are based on temperature, humidity, and so on. The horses are subjected to very thorough veterinary checks before they leave; along the way they are observed by the judges. At a midpoint they are held for several minutes while their pulse and respiration are taken and dehydration tests are performed. After the ride or drive, they undergo even more rigorous checks. The winning horse is the one in the best condition. With a score in the high 90s, he will look, after, say, fifty miles, as if he had not yet left the barn.

The horse who almost killed me is seventeen. His mother was a Standardbred who had failed at the track and fallen on bad times. We took her out of a deplorable situation one bitter January day, and trailered her down to Princeton, where I was to teach for a semester in the creative writing program. The mare, then a four-year-old, had been confined for months in a space barely big enough to turn around in. Her front hooves had grown out and around her shoes. She had lost so much muscle tone that her body felt like an immense Jell-O mold. Once in Holmdel, New Jersey, in a forty-acre field shared with several Welsh ponies, she relearned how to gallop and cavort. At the end of the term we returned to New Hampshire to begin her career as a distance horse under saddle.

I soon discovered her fatal flaw. In a group of horses dispatched at one-minute intervals she became increasingly agitated, indeed uncontrollable from the saddle. "If you'd a' breathed on her belly she'd a' gone over," an equestrian friend remarked, observing her rearing in place. I learned not to put my toe in the stirrup until my number was called. Then, as she felt me shift my weight, bringing my right leg down on her right side, we would set out at the ground-eating trot Standardbreds are famous for.

The mare's name was Genesis. Her firstborn son we called Deuteronomy, Deuter, or The Dude for short. I was the first thing he saw when he slipped out of his mother. He stood almost immediately that cold March night, a wide-eyed and stiff-legged chestnut with a white star and two white hind socks. Although he grew into his head and ears, at that moment he looked like a miniature draft horse.

Privileged from the outset, he was easy to live with and easy to train. He bonded with humans, invariably whinnying back when either of us went out to the pasture to call him. Our only gelding, he observed his place in the pack, deferring always to the imperious mares, and casually accepted the company of our dogs, who often travelled at his heels. He only took offense when the youngest, a little white foundling mutt, would squirm into a culvert on one side of the road and emerge from it on the other as we trotted by; this called for a vigorous sidestep and a little grunt before Deuter recovered his composure.

He loved distance work, attacked the hills of New England as if they were mere hummocks, and was comfortable in a group of horses. Horse people in general liked his agreeable nature and sturdy build. They said things like, "He has a very large motor in the hind end," and "Well, he's a little over-endowed in the ears department but he sure can cover ground." He was the horse I had waited for all my life.

By the time he was about ten, arthritis was making long hours in the saddle painful for me and I reluctantly switched from riding horses to driving them. We began with a lightweight two-seater phaeton made of ash. Because of our hilly terrain we had a hydraulic brake installed so that the driver could hold the weight of the cart back from the horse's hind end while going downhill, a great boon in distance work. A little later, we acquired a small sleigh, a replica of the famous Portland cutter once used by rural doctors to make their rounds in winter.

All four of our horses made the transition from work-

ing under saddle to going in harness, some more read-
ily than others. Our youngest, a three-quarters Arabian
mare of impeccable bloodlines, spent the better part of
her fourth year protesting that shafts must never touch
her sides, but eventually grew into a very correct driving horse.

The genes from his Arabian sire combined with his
Standardbred half to make The Dude a natural harness
horse. He could travel all day at a steady open trot
without apparent effort. On woods roads he was sane
and clever about negotiating the twists and turns. Out
on asphalt he was never entirely relaxed but gradually
learned to put up with traffic whizzing past. We brought
home some blue ribbons—typically, driving event ribbons are long and flowing affairs—and proudly hung
them in the living room, temporarily obliterating two
pen-and-ink drawings by Boston artist friends, Harold
Tovich and Barbara Swan. Barbara's are the originals of
pen-and-ink drawings she had done to accompany some
of the poems in my collection, *Up Country*, which won
the Pulitzer Prize in 1973.

We also attended some sleigh rallies and then moved
on to combined-driving events, where obedience, speed,
and lightness and ease of movement are key requisites.
Deuter had incurred a strained ligament on the final

stretch of the hundred-mile drive and I felt that he needed a break from distance work. In combined driving he enlarged his vocabulary to embrace several new verbal commands: "slow trot," "working," "trot on," "back," and "come up." Because he was so responsive to my voice, he scored well in dressage.

In addition to dressage, the other two phases of a combined-driving show involve weaving between an often tricky obstacle course of cones in correct numerical order without dislodging any of the tennis balls perched atop the cones, and traversing a marathon that typically concludes with five to seven "hazards." Deeming this term too fraught with danger, the American Driving Society seeks to replace it with the word "obstacle," but among drivers, hazard is the common word still. Hazards frequently involve crossing brooks and streams, covered or other bridges, and making tight turns up and down hill as well.

We had now reached a level of competition in which my two-seater phaeton was no longer safe. It's a road cart, great on the straightaway, but tippy on the slant. At this juncture, I bought the marathon four-wheeler. The navigator on the rear step provides ballast for the carriage as it swings around sharp corners, negotiating the hazards at a speed commensurate with the whip's and the horse's ability. For three halcyon seasons with this vehicle I worked hard to improve my driving skills and bring Deuter to ever-higher levels of performance. My navigator and I went to clinics and horse trials; we trailered north and south to adjoining states. Still a jock, I was so caught up in the competitive driving world that I turned down all summer poetry seminar and reading options between May 1 and October 1. My hubris knew no bounds. If only it had been otherwise! If only some Cassandra had whispered in my ear.

July 23

The family assembles. Our son Danny, who lives about thirty miles from our farm, raced up the highway from the southern part of the state where he had been blissfully reading the *New York Times*, a luxury in rural New Hampshire, while his Saab was being lubricated.

"You never saw a car come off a lift so fast," he tells me long after the fact. Notorious for crowding the speed limit as a matter of course, he says, "I more than exceeded it; I abolished it."

Daughter Judith, press officer for the United Nations

High Commission for Refugees in Geneva, Switzerland, took the first available flight, arrived in Boston within thirty-six hours of my debacle, rented a car, and hurried north. Our older daughter, Jane, in close touch by phone, came a few days later from San Francisco. Dan's wife Libby came evenings; after some discussion, she brought their eight-year-old son with her.

"I wasn't exactly scared," Noah told me months later. "I mean, I didn't know who you were, you looked so awful on the bed. But I asked Mom when you would be Ga [the name he calls me] again and she said it would take a while but it would happen."

July 24

Everything is relative in the unnatural environment of the Intensive Care Unit; after a few days I am deemed well enough to be moved upstairs, to the Neuroscience Unit, where the spinal cord and brain injuries are looked after. I am moved in my Roto Rest bed, a wide flat pad. My head and neck are in traction, and each limb is pinned flat, as the bed rotates constantly to keep fluid from collecting in my lungs and prevent pneumonia. I am not yet attached to the halo vest. To my mild surprise, all the family members come and go in a sort of hallucinatory chain. I marvel that I was not astonished by their sudden appearances. It did not occur to me at the time that this was like the convening of relatives at a deathbed.

July 26

I rely on Judith for the following account, because whatever bits and pieces of it I remember have detached themselves like floaters across the retina. When the young resident makes his rounds—it is a Sunday morning and none of the neurologists is present—he finds I have lost all neurological response in my extremities. Was I conscious? Did I read the alarm on the faces of my daughters and son? Did I realize it was the probable death of my arms and legs they were mourning? The resident sends me down for another MRI to see if there is new bleeding in the spinal cord.

I, who mistrust even inoffensive public elevators, am terrified of MRIs; I am terrified of tightly enclosed spaces. Today, though, I am so heavily medicated that I am almost fearless. The inside of this MRI machine is tiled white, like a urinal. My earlier experience had been of entombment in a black tunnel. That procedure was performed at the request of the rheumatologist who

31

monitors my polymyalgia rheumatica. I only got through it by reciting heavily cadenced and tightly rhymed poems out of my memory bank.

Whenever I teach graduate students in a master of fine arts program, I require them to memorize thirty or so lines of traditional poetry every week. This does not make me popular initially. "I'm doing you a favor," I tell them. "I'm giving you an internal library to draw on when you are taken political prisoner."

My own internal library is full of the poems I fell in love with in adolescence: Edna St. Vincent Millay, Longfellow, Wordsworth, A. E. Housman. Housman, author of *A Shropshire Lad*, composed brief melancholic verses about failed love and imminent death that appealed to my romantic nature, and I acquired these poems in my teens as if by osmosis. His trimeters really thump along with the racketing of the MRI machine: "With rue my heart is laden / For golden friends I had; / For many a rose-lip't maiden / And many a lightfoot lad."

Later the same day, a woman neurologist spends an hour examining me and another hour on the phone consulting her colleagues. She concludes that swelling in the intact spinal cord is responsible for the neurological change and orders massive doses of steroids. In cases where the spinal cord has been mashed or nicked, paralysis ensues at varying levels. If the cord has been severed, there is resultant loss of function in the sites governed by the injury.

("That was quite a ding your spinal cord took," Kathy told me later. I still have total amnesia for the moment I was thrown out of the carriage, and no great desire to retrieve the memory.)

July 27

Neurological response has returned to my arms. A volleyball team of orthopedists and orthopedic residents assembles at my bedside. Even in my morphine-induced haze, I resent the fact that they poke, prod, and squeeze, and speak to each other but never directly to me. When they leave, my nurse has a few things to say on the subject of orthopedists. I treasure this one: "Orthopedic surgeons are like little boys with Meccano toys [the British equivalent of our Erector sets]. They like to take things apart and put them together again. They never have to look people in the eye."

Today I am released from traction, and the halo vest (which together with the bird cage contraption immobilizes my head, neck and shoulders) is put on. I am moved onto a regular hospital bed. The various IV lines are removed. A nurse cranks the back of the bed up a little, and for the first time in a week I see something other than the ceiling. Danny sits beside me feeding me ice chips one at a time. He is very tactful with the chips; I can't tolerate having anything held up to my face without my express consent. Even this hand that I know and love is a menace. He waits until I signal with a small nod, then offers me another sliver of ice from the plastic spoon.

July 28

The doctors seem unable to decide whether I belong in Neuroscience with the other spinal cord injuries, or in Orthopedics, with all the broken bones. Finally, at the start of week two, I am moved down to the Orthopedic Ward.

Here, they put me into a reclining chair twice a day. I am a marionette; my arms and legs have to be moved by others, I am turned on my bed every two hours. Of course I have no bladder or bowel control either, and am invaded by a Foley catheter. For the first month each meal is an enormous undertaking, for both the feeder and the fed. My older daughter spends an hour and a half spooning a cup of soup and a small container of yogurt into me. Even though I know I have to eat, I feel attacked by the spoon each time it approaches my lips. At this point, I don't think much about the ironic role reversal that has taken place in my life. Infantilized, I am tended now in shifts by my anxious offspring. My thinking, mercifully, is still clouded. The drugs, when they come, release me further. Emily Dickinson's "Plank in Reason" having broken, I travel backward out of my animality into a sort of suspended bodilessness.

I'm not up to solid food yet. Although the hospital menu offers lots of choices, what arrives on my tray goes back largely untouched. Mostly what I get to eat are cream soups Judith makes from the beets, potatoes, spinach, carrots direct-seeded in the garden in late spring, and the cauliflower and broccoli that I lovingly set out in May from seeds started on the living room windowsills. Everything continues to burgeon while I lie here vegetating. The corn is waist-high, the tomatoes are climbing their trellises.

Keeping the garden going becomes for the family a way of keeping me going. Every morning Judith climbs the hill above the farmhouse to where my fenced garden is situated, just below the pond. Everything here is grown organically. The plants thrive in a soil heavily amended with rotted horse manure and are mulched with spoiled hay. The walkways are papered with old grain bags and then covered with pine needles. It has taken years to achieve this orderly oasis, which somehow compensates for my disorderly desk drawers and the chaos of my closet. If the weather has been dry, Victor waters the garden from the pond in the late afternoon, when the sun has dropped behind the trees.

My passion for the garden is rather like my passion for our horses. In addition to the provender it supplies, there is its dailiness, its innate discipline. Horses must be fed and watered, groomed and inspected on a regular basis to check for scrapes, punctures, problems of whatever sort. The garden, too, exacts the same attention. After two or three days of rain, slugs may magically appear, working their way through a row of lettuces. I pick them off, slime and all, and hurl them over the fence, where the birds will make quick work of them. Cabbage worms, tomato hornworms, cutworms, squash borers meet the same fate, though in truth we seldom encounter any of these.

In my suburban past, I had only a few self-seeding petunias and cosmos to deal with. The yard was shady; dandelions dotted the grass. To my indifferent eye, it looked adequately tidy. But when we acquired the farm, I gradually began to see another landscape entirely.

Wild asparagus appeared, waving their ferny fronds in unexpected places. In a small sunny clearing, rhubarb emerged. Garlic chives sent up little white blossoms along the house foundation and great unkillable clumps of chives with fat purple blooms ran rampant around them. Clusters of what resembled sunflowers proved to be edible Jerusalem artichokes. The first time Victor mowed the area we were slowly restoring to lawn, the wonderful pungency of fresh thyme arose from the nubbly "grass."

All of these unknowns drove me to wildflower and garden handbooks. My rural education began in books, continued with seed catalogs, my favorite January reading, and was helped along by Victor's willingness to double-dig the soil, loosen huge rocks with a crowbar, haul them out by brute strength and/or chain attached to a come-along attached to a nearby tree. A chemical engineer by profession but with a handyman's innate ability to cope with every conceivable problem, it was Victor who fenced our first tiny vegetable garden with chicken wire to resist the marauding woodchucks. It was he who shot half a dozen of the mighty population that had laid claim to this derelict property over the six tenantless years before we bought it. We both took aim at porcupines that first season. I

suffered enough pangs of guilt for both of us murder-
ers but consoled myself with the knowledge that up
until recent times the state paid a five-dollar bounty on
ears from what are still known quaintly as quilly pigs.

Over the years, the vegetable garden evolved into
two separate entities: mine, abutting the pond, and
Victor's, overlooking it from the upper pasture. To be
candid, I think one of the tactics that contributed to the
success of our marriage was that we always compart-
mentalized our professional lives much as we've sec-
tioned off the vegetable gardens. I never proofread or
paragraphed his technical papers prior to their publi-
cation, and he seldom read any of my poems or essays
until they appeared in print. But we knew how to offer
sympathy and encouragement; we each cultivated an
instinct for when to speak up or stay silent; each of us
had a good idea of when to fix a bloody mary or a
scotch on the rocks for the other, or when to pack up a
picnic and get the kids out of the house to give the
other weary parent some surcease.

The asparagus bed is entirely Victor's. He tends,
feeds, and is vigilant for the first sprouts. (He is a little
deficient in the weeding department, so his asparagus
patch looks rather like my desk, an area of fecund dis-
order.) When the bed truly begins to bear, we eat aspara-

gus nightly and gratefully. In the rest of his space, he used to grow corn, but it did poorly in only partial sun and haphazardly mulched; it seems much happier in my raised beds. I was more than willing to cede him winter squash in return, as these love to sprawl and run and I could not contain them. He plants acorn, Hubbard, and butternut, and a few celebratory pumpkins for decoration. Once squash plants begin to spread, their massive leaves cover the ground and crowd out any weeds that preexisted, making cucurbits, the family that includes cucumbers, squash, gourds, and other trailing plants, the vegetable of choice for this gardener. Two autumns ago he harvested seventy-five butternut squash from his shady patch. We fobbed them off on the mail carrier, the UPS driver, the farrier, the driver of the propane gas delivery truck, and every hapless visitor who came up our hill. Luckily, germination rates were down the following year.

This season, it is Judith who daily inspects my seven thirty-foot-long raised beds for insect depredation (thanks to companionate planting and volunteer dill, which hosts beneficial parasitic wasps, there seldom is any). She climbs over the stile, a horse-mounting block on either side of the four-foot fence. Whatever needs picking—broccoli, cauliflower, early green beans, lettuce, radishes, the last of the peas—she takes down to the house to be dealt with. The surplus is blanched and frozen for the winter ahead. The tomatoes are not quite ready; the corn, cucumbers, and summer squashes are still ripening, but soon there will be that gratifying mountain of veggies, the benevolent tyranny I always strive to stay abreast of, pickling, canning, and freezing. A poem of mine in praise of gardens ends:

> O children, my wayward jungly dears
> you are all to be celebrated
> plucked, transplanted, tilled under, resurrected here
> —even the lowly despised
> purslane, chickweed, burdock, poke, wild poppies.
> For all of you, whether eaten or extirpated
> I plan to spend the rest of my life on my knees.

July 29

Judith arranges to spend the night on a cot in my room, having been unable to locate a night-sitter. Ever since I moved out of the Neuroscience Unit, where nurses stayed in the room twenty-four hours a day, the family has been hiring freelance women to spend the night sitting in the chair in my room. I am terrified of being left alone; I cannot ring for the nurse, or take a sip of water unassisted. In fact, I cannot change position unassisted, even by an inch or two. In my total dependency, I have become the child and Judith the parent. Ordinarily, I would hate this state of affairs.

Instead, I am hugely grateful for her presence. Do I know she has taken an unpaid leave from her very demanding UN job to look after me? My barely sentient life feels like a very long and lonely voyage, perhaps one that will never end. Desperate for another human presence, I am salved to have this daughter mother me. It is a humbling experience to be reduced to infancy, to be the helpless girl-child who calls in the night, and who is reassured by the mother she comes so unerringly to love.

Last night's sitter was something of a disaster. She announced at the outset, "My brother died in this very room," thereby establishing a lugubrious tone for the long night ahead.

With Judith, I watch television for the first time. Although I don't remember the substance, she tells me we watched a National Geographic special on bears and a feature about child prostitutes in Thailand. The children spoke Thai and subtitles were provided in English. Apparently I reacted to the subtitles. What a huge turning point this is! Up until this moment, no one knew if I could read; there was a strong possibility I might never regain the brain function necessary to do so. Now, even though I am severely handicapped, words, my beloved instruments, have swum back into my ken.

August 2

Today is Victor's seventy-seventh birthday. I am only dimly aware of the occasion because all three children leave the hospital early to prepare a semblance of a birthday dinner. An old friend and fellow poet drives over from the university where she is teaching a summer school course in creative writing, to pass the afternoon and evening with me. Of course I know she is there; we have a long and enduring relationship. At the same time, I see her as an apparition of sorts, a ghost flitting across my consciousness. I am not capable of any sustained conversation.

August 4

Plants and flowers usurp every flat surface in my cubicle. Judith threatens to redistribute the wealth to flowerless patients. Here my two lives intersect: floral tributes from the Academy of American Poets and the *New York Times Book Review* abut those sent by Acme Carriage Works and the Green Mountain Horse Association.

Every day Victor brings in piles of cards and E-mail messages. He reads them to me and stuffs them back in his briefcase. I fret that they are accumulating unanswered on my desk or his; how will I ever catch up? (I need not have worried. Victor has been indefatigable, keeping in touch with all inquiries by phone, E-mail, or letter. After the fact, I learn about his long, optimistic responses to close friends, former students, my editor. I am his project; staying in touch with the world beyond the hospital is part of that project. It is also his way of fighting back the demon of depression, an omnipresent menace hanging over both of us. It is uncertain whether I will ever walk again or be able to use my arms; possibly I will require constant custodial care. Looking back over his E-mails to my editor, I read: "I have engaged an architect to prepare for modification of our house to facilitate the long-term living arrangements. This is to combine bedroom, study, bath and patio or porch all on one floor.")

For the first few weeks, then, everything was in doubt. The medical record reports an initial diagnosis of quadriparesis. It is typical of Victor's problem-solving mentality that he promptly set about preparing to bring home a paralyzed wife. He was horrified, he was saddened. But the word "depressed" with its connotations of gloom and apathy does not apply.

A further concern is my calendar. I have already missed two readings and there are several other bookings in this month alone. I never cancel a commitment, even if I am running a fever. (Here, too, Victor has taken hold, cancelling everything through the month of December, in most cases by phone, expatiating fully on my accident, thereby rousing everyone to send cards and letters.)

August 7

Judith is startled to read my name on a white board in the hallway as scheduled for transfer in three days to a rehabilitation hospital fifty miles away. No one in the family has been consulted about the move but it will be a step in the direction of improved mobility. Although I am not anxious to leave what has become a familiar haven, I realize that the transfer will ease the travel burden on family members. In the new facility, I will be only twenty minutes from home.

August 10

Two uniformed attendants come for me with a gurney and transfer me into the waiting ambulance. Everything takes place with me lying supine and uninvolved. At least there are no sirens. The upper landscape flickers past. I look at the treetops, bathed in noon sunlight, with the curiosity of an alien. The route we traverse is one I have travelled dozens of times in our big Ford pickup, hauling two horses in the attached trailer to a clinic or show, or just to pleasure-ride with friends in another area. Even though the outside air does not touch my skin today, I can imagine the touch and smell of it.

At first I am alone in a room in the rehab facility. My call button to summon a nurse is a soft square reserved for neurological patients because it responds to the very weak pressure I can muster with my left hand. (My right hand is still useless.) Alas, I can never find this square. Without the means to summon help I am suffused with claustrophobia. Finally one of the staff fastens it to a thin hardcover copy of *The History of Modern Art*—what prior patient left this behind?—which she wedges between my body and the bed rail. Now, even with my very limited sensation, I can distinguish the square from the bedsheet.

At night an aide packs my feet into Multi Podus boots. Fleece-lined, with great metal bars on the bottom, they are designed to prevent foot-drop in the immobilized. It seems that all the spinal-cord injured are required to set sail at night in these contraptions. In addition I must wear high white elastic stockings to reduce swelling, improve circulation, and guard against blood clots.

Every two hours someone comes to change my position ever so slightly. (My most vivid recollection is of one especially strict nurse standing at the foot of my bed, which is bathed in full electric light at 2 A.M., shaking her finger, saying, "She's only allowed to lie on her back, put her back on her back," as my feet cramp up from the confinement of the boots. After four or five nights of this routine I refuse to wear them. "Just write on my chart: 'Patient refused to wear her boots,'" I say to the night nurse, and nobody ever hassles me about them again.)

Whoever makes the 2 A.M. check seems to delight in changing the date on the wall calendar with a gratifying rip of paper. I think: another day down the drain! Some one of the many doctors who have come and gone in my room has told me that I will be confined in the halo for eight to twelve weeks. I am absolutely positive that I will be healed in eight weeks. Every day that goes by moves me one day closer to freedom.

August 11

Three weeks have gone by since the accident. This is my first full day in the rehab hospital. A procession of nurses and aides and social workers files in and out to introduce themselves. Everybody wants to know how I broke my neck. I say merely that I had a carriage-driving accident. The social worker questions me further: "But how do you *feel* about your accident?" Although shaken, my tactic with her is not to reply. (In the subsequent medical report I am said to be "slightly confused, unable to relate history well.")

When I retell this incident to Judith she says it reminds her of an interview she saw recently with an Iraqi Kurdish refugee who had arrived, via Turkey, by small boat on a Greek island. His wife and baby had drowned during the voyage. The television reporter shoved a microphone into his face and asked him: "How do you feel about your decision to flee Iraq, now that your wife and child have died?"

How I *feel* about my accident defies description. I don't let myself come close to reviewing the actual event, except to think over and over that it would have been better to have been killed outright. Yes, my wonderful family would have grieved, but eventually they would have gotten on with their lives. Yes, Victor, above all others, would have been terribly bereft, but with his proactive and optimistic nature, he too would have picked up the pieces of his life and gotten on with it. Perhaps he would sell the farm, move to the seacoast which he loves, and resume sailing. Possibly he would go back to the city with its subways and skyscrapers and museums and theaters—for aren't these the things I lured him away from? How I *feel* about my accident is quite simply that I screwed up everybody's life by living through it.

August 12

After a day of interrogation about the accident, I summon the courage to ask what happened to my horse after he threw me out of the carriage and bolted around the field. (I don't yet know that he actually tore back through the entry gate and raced two miles down the state highway before one of the groundskeepers caught up with him.) Victor tells me that he was unharmed: "Not a scratch on him." I picture Deuter out in the back pasture, calmly grazing with the rest of the herd, while I have yet to get onto my feet. I don't know if he was still attached to the carriage when he was saved, or if he had managed to tear loose from the harness. I'm not ready yet to ask these questions. But having pictured my favorite horse downed in a tangle of leather and shaft poles, a leg broken, his hip gashed open by the singletree, blood pouring from his nose as he struggles and struggles to rise, after having pictured the call to the sheriff, the vet, the state police, somebody, anybody with a pistol to put him out of his misery, my relief, even gratitude, is prodigious. I love this guy. He and I are still alive.

Although I am unaware of the purpose of his visit, a cherubic-looking, somewhat rotund young doctor stops by to see me today. He has a pleasing, sympathetic manner, and as he repeats the usual neurological tests for my reflexes (exaggerated), grasp strength (minimal), and pinprick sensation (reduced), we chat for perhaps twenty minutes. Reading the record after my discharge, I discover that this is a neuropsychiatric evaluation to determine my "cognitive and emotional state." I am said to have told him I am feeling "whiffly" around the edges. The word I was reaching for is "squiffy," but it too is absent from the dictionary. I am said to be fairly optimistic about the future, have not been having any crying jags, and do not describe myself as feeling hopeless or helpless.

This bravado is my badge of honor. No one on the staff is going to find me out, except by stealth or mischance. Just as Victor used to say of me when I whined, writing recommendations for others, that I never had a Guggenheim, had never been to a writers' colony, "You are your own MacDowell," so I must be my own salvation. "All right, I say, I'll save myself," Sexton says in a poem. I am living that line.

August 13

Eva, my first walker, is big, blue, and sturdy with a sort of jack that adjusts up or down to fit the user. I am incredulous; my two therapists expect me to rise from the bed and actually stand? I am like an early toddler, drunkenly clinging to my Eva governess, finally daring to push one foot and then the other forward three inches. What a miracle it seems! I am upright, no longer a total prisoner of the bed, even though I am still dragging my Foley catheter everywhere. Learning to toddle, not yet toilet-trained, skinny (I have lost at least twenty pounds), I am expected to agree with my family, who all say how lucky I am to be alive. But that's not really what I feel. I feel infantilized, outraged, furious at my fate.

August 14

After a few days alone, I acquire my first roommate, who is recovering from her second hip replacement. My fears of having to share this space with some dotty old lady are misplaced; I am the dotty old lady and she is the healthier, more mobile one. She and her husband cheer me on as I learn to transfer from bed to wheelchair, an aide on either side.

She goes down to the dining room for meals. Mine arrive on a tray and I have to wait for an aide or a family member to feed me. I cannot open the half-pint milk carton; I cannot poke a straw into the little orange juice container. My left hand struggles to fasten on a spoon, lift one slice of banana to my mouth, then falters, unable to complete the task.

August 15

My first trip down to the gym, via wheelchair. It's a great open space with windows on two sides beckoning the viewer to shrubbery, flowers, grass, and a grid of surfaces designed to test the balance skills of the newly walking—bricks, a boardwalk, gravelly asphalt, ramps, and sturdy stairs with double banisters. I think to myself that I'll never be up to these challenges.

"You'll walk," the therapists tell me. "You will positively absolutely learn to walk and we're here to teach you." My initial chore is to learn to rise from the wheelchair and grab onto Eva. It's all so hard and so tiring. I wish everyone would go away and leave me alone.

I am to have at least two sessions each day of physical and occupational therapy. The PTs work with legs, endurance, and balance. The OTs work on arms, hands, and fingers. My range of motion is almost nonexistent and I can hold neither a cup nor a spoon. In addition, I am assigned a speech therapist to assess my mild aphasia, which, along with some retrograde amnesia, is thought to be a residual of the concussion.

The two PTs who work with me are kind but demanding. Sue is tall and slim, somewhat reserved, very well spoken. She started in medical school and then changed direction. Wendy, a high school dropout, is stocky, blond, and tough. Her attitude is no-nonsense, let's get it done, and I will never lie to you. Both of them seem to think I can perform what are to me impossible feats of endurance. They chivvy and push me; I must. To walk forty steps with one of them holding me up by my voyaging belt—a broad woven band worn around the waist—and the other on the alert to catch me if I stumble becomes a heroic journey. My halo is no excuse; they've dealt with dozens of spinal cord patients in halos who have learned to stand up straight, keep their balance, and swing their arms as they walk. "Come on, let's go!" they say. And go again. After every session I am wheeled back upstairs, collapse on my bed, and drift into uneasy sleep, only to be fetched awake by an aide for the next session.

Transferred from wheelchair to bed, I have just dozed off when the speech therapist arrives to investigate my deficiencies. My speech appears haltingly slow to me; some of my words feel slurred. These problems, she assures me, will pass. She hazards the opinion that I am only conscious of these marginal changes because of my past history of speaking in public. More troubling are the gaps—words I cannot find. "Give me an example," she says.

"The word for the thing you turn eggs over with. Or pancakes."

"Think of another way to describe it," she urges. "What is it made of? Is it thin or thick?"

"It's made of metal," I say petulantly, "it's broad, with cutouts. And it flexes." We wallow around in this conundrum for a few minutes until suddenly the word appears. "Spatula!" I say.

Equally troubling to me is the way my voice sounds. I think I am slurring my words, as if I have had too much to drink. I enunciate elaborately, but when I do this, I feel I am talking too slowly, like a recent stroke victim. My therapist explains that I lost consciousness for several minutes following the accident and the concussion I sustained may be responsible for these side effects. She finds them barely perceptible. Much as I want to be reassured, I don't quite trust this assessment.

As we get to know each other, I begin to look forward to her comforting presence each day, even if our session only lasts twenty minutes or so. She is reading my essays and stories in *Women, Animals, and Vegetables,* having found a copy in her local library. Our conversations are inconsequential but they help to restore my self esteem; I begin to reabsorb the being I was before the accident. Even in my reduced, supine position, I am not quite a total prisoner. I am capable of sustained thought. I can communicate that thought.

August 16

Family members take turns wheeling me out of doors, two pillows on my lap to support my still nearly dead arms. I rediscover what every infant knows: the joys of perambulation. I give in to the sensation of forward motion, bright sunlight, the line of trees that I can barely see because of the halo restraints, and the comforting vibration of the wheelchair on pavement. Every mother remembers tucking a fussy infant or toddler, fiercely resisting sleep, into a pram or a stroller and wheeling her down the block to Nirvana.

August 17

Judith arrives today with her laptop computer. Actually, she's brought it along a few times before this and used it to catch up on UN business while I attend PT or doze, exhausted, after a learning-to-walk session. But today she announces her intent.

"Mom, you're always saying that if you're a writer nothing is ever all for nothing. I'm going to take dictation, starting now. Let's write about this." She gestures around the room. "I know you can do it. We'll get an article out of it! You talk and I'll type."

And so it begins. From this day on we find some place to hide for forty-five minutes or an hour, or even a little longer. I do indeed talk. Everything comes pouring out: the grief, anger, frustration, fear—not in these abstract words, but in the feelings they evoke. I particularize as best I can.

We try to keep this activity secret. I don't want to trade on my status as a writer and I especially don't want any prying eyes to see what we're doing. Judith is very discreet. She prints out pages at home and brings them to me to read the next day. I can't even separate the pages myself with my numb fingers; she turns them for me one at a time.

August 18

Every morning just getting dressed is an ordeal. Socks and shoes are still beyond me, though I am firmly urged to try, every day, to accomplish something more on my own. My arms can't make their way into armholes without assistance. I am counselled always to begin with the "weak" arm—one never says "bad"— then insert head through neck hole, then worm the "better" arm in place. Judith has supplied me with various size 22 V-neck pullovers off the rack at Lane Bryant to fit over the ever-menacing spires of the halo. Anything wide enough to go over my head rack is also wide enough to start slipping off my shoulders. But since I have not yet confronted myself in a mirror, I am not fully aware of how ragged I look.

It is actually quite easy to avoid facing my own image in the rehab hospital. My room has one mirror, placed directly over the sink; I consider myself fortunate that I can't see into it from the wheelchair. Even though Victor assures me that my black eye is gone and the purple contusions on my cheekbone have faded, I have only to look at my right forearm (restricted by the halo, I can't see any higher than my elbow) to infer that the rest of me is still mottled black and blue. I was always on good terms with my body, even as it aged, alluding to it in a poem as "Body, old partner, Old Paint. . . ." Now it is an encumbrance and I shrink from it.

In the gym the OTs work my nearly useless arms as I lie on a mat. My right upper arm was run over by a carriage wheel, its imprint, they tell me, as visible as a tattoo. (At this point I choose not to inquire further, but conclude that Deuter must have swerved to avoid stepping on me and thus pulled the marathon vehicle over my right side.) After the mat session of passive exercise I am required to sit at a table and manipulate any number of children's toys: pegs, blocks, and a clay-like substance called Thera-Putty, which I am to roll out and pinch into ridges using my thumb and forefinger.

This is a daunting task, one I detest. It makes me face up to all my weaknesses and accept these fingers in their dormant if not permanently dead state. The fourth and fifth fingers on my right hand have neither sensation nor function. My wrist and forearm appear to be veiled in some gauzy material. My upper arm pains me continually. It is a relief when the session ends. (My extreme pessimism about my right hand is to persist; even after I am able, clumsily and with many errors, to use a keyboard again, I cling morbidly to the notion that the damage cannot be repaired.)

Now that I'm in the gym daily for long periods, I revert to people-watching. In airports across the country I've detached myself from my book to study hybrid human arrangements flowing past me on the moving sidewalks or in and out of the little eateries that dot the corridors. Here in the gym I pull back into myself and study my fellow beings. It's a scene out of a Fellini movie: a young and beautiful paraplegic woman pulling herself up on the parallel bars; an elderly man befuddled by his stroke, desperately trying to follow the nurse's commands that he tell her when her moving finger crosses his line of vision; people with hip replacements and knee replacements leaning on their walkers, and single and double amputees scooting nimbly around in their chairs.

There's my roommate, who has graduated to a walker with wheels in front and is making her second circle around the gym. I see my halo partner, who rolled his car trying to avoid a deer and fractured his neck a little lower down than my fracture. We are the cripples that people in Wal-Mart or J. C. Penney gawk at, as if we were mentally compromised as well. Yet in here we are citizens of one world, carefully tended and turned, fed and watered, sheltered from further vicissitude.

August 19

The garden is now at its peak. The early corn is ready and Judith is determined I am not to be deprived of tasting the fruit of my labors. She arrives with two fat ears. I inspect them critically—are the kernels filled out? any insect damage at the tip?—and pronounce them perfect. It's been three months from date of birth, as it were.

On May 15 I performed my annual ritual: I started 250 corn seeds—half an early yellow variety and half a late white—in plant cells on the glassed-in front porch. By June 6, my seventy-third birthday, they were six inches high. One by one I set them out in the garden, triangulated at ten-inch intervals. Two weeks later, the soil having reached its peak temperature, I hilled up around each shoot, papered the planted beds with old issues of the *New York Times Book Review*, the perfect width to fit between seedlings, and mulched with old hay. I go through this finicky procedure of hilling up and tucking in every year. Corn is shallowly rooted and will topple over in a summer storm unless supported. But once I get this far, no further care is required until the silks on the early corn turn from milk color to a sort of burgundy and the elongated ears swell, as they now have, to a desired plumpness.

Judith cooks the two ears in their husks in the microwave in the Hospitality Suite. She serves them to me on a paper plate with butter and salt. Lifting the first ear to my mouth is a Herculean task; my right hand is still too wobbly and weak to provide adequate support. But the first bite brings back to me the sought-after sweetness lodged in these tender yet crunchy kernels. I offer Judith a bite and she agrees. Corn snobs to the death, we smugly concur that you can't buy this flavor at any market.

Each day now, either Judith or Victor deposits a basket of vegetables at the nurses' desk or in the gym office to be divided among the aides and therapists. I am a celebrity by way of my vegetable garden. Recipients consult me: what is the name of this funny-looking yellow thing (pattypan summer squash)? what are these thick leaves (New Zealand spinach) and how do you cook them? what do you do with these purple and white balls (kohlrabi)? And for the first time ever, we have no zucchini glut since every single self-satisfied zucchini goes home with an employee.

August 21

Today is my first try to get off the Foley catheter. I will be catheterized every six hours if I am unable to void on my own. At least the every-other-6 A.M. suppository routine is over and done with. ("Suppository" was another of the words I searched for but could not find on my own.) After this entire month of infantilism, I will never take bowel control for granted again.

By evening it is apparent that the experiment isn't working. The bladder ultrasound shows that I am unable to empty this organ and the Foley catheter is reinstalled. I feel relieved of an obligation I could not live up to, but ignominiously defeated at the same time. I am back on antibiotics to counteract an ongoing bladder infection. What if I never recover the sensation that will allow me to pee on my own? How will I handle the rest of my life if I am always to be threaded with a catheter and dependent on pills?

August 23

A pattern of visits has developed. Either Victor or Judith comes at noon to get me fed. Danny, ever the faithful son, comes almost every evening. Sometimes his wife Libby accompanies him. Sometimes she comes alone, bringing expensive emollients manufactured from royal bee jelly or special herbs, and spends an hour massaging my icy feet, my numb hands. It is the only time I experience a glimmer of feeling in them. I love having her give me this gift of touch.

August 24

I get my toes back. Up until now I have been walking on dead feet that feel like cold, wet pancakes. My toes feel swollen and alien to me. My ankles are not swollen but I perceive them as huge balloons. It is terrifying to flex the ankle joint, but in physical therapy I do so under instruction and miraculously my foot does not fall off. My view of my lower extremities is impeded by the halo, which prevents me from bending beyond the fixed point at which the bottom ends of the halo uprights dig into my pectoral muscles. (It will be months before these deep bruises fade.)

My roommate is cleared to go home today, but I am the one who is given a going-away present. Her husband arrives with an enormous glass jar full of cashew nuts. "High protein for vegetarians," he says.

Judith brings him a basket of beets from my garden in exchange. They spend a long time discussing methods of pickling.

My vegetarianism is an ongoing issue; I must eat more protein, I am told. I need the iron found in red meat. But I can't bring myself to backslide. As it is, I do eat fish, something I am not proud of. I think of Thoreau, who writes in *Walden*: "I cannot fish without falling a little in self-respect." A docked fish flopping about as it suffocates to death is hardly different from the blow to the head that kills the used-up dairy cow destined to become McDonald's hamburger. And then there is the truth that children tell. I remember our daughter Jane at age five asking, as her father forced lobsters into a pot of boiling water: "How do we know they're not screaming lobster screams and we just can't hear them?"

August 25

I am X-rayed at weekly intervals. A portable X-ray machine is wheeled into my room from a nearby radiology clinic. Every week I am told there is no sign of healing yet. At the end of week five it is discovered that the odontoid fracture has slipped out of position. The doctor in charge at the rehab hospital confines me to bed rest with bathroom privileges only. "Probably," he says, "surgery is indicated."

I am scheduled to go back to the critical care hospital the next day to see the orthopedic surgeon. What a disaster! Five whole weeks of healing wasted! Judith and I are both frantic. Victor has gone to Cape Cod for a three-day respite with Danny and his family. Even though I am terrified of the terra incognita ahead, I implore Judith not to notify them. It will only spread the anguish around, like runny jam on toast. We agree to wait until after tomorrow's events.

After a number of tries to get in touch with the surgeon himself, Judith reaches the resident in orthopedic surgery by phone. He assures her that such dislocations are not uncommon and that surgery is almost definitely not indicated. We both breathe easier. But I feel I have fallen to the lower depths. What else can happen to me? Why didn't I die on the spot and get it over with?

Each of us, true to form, is trying to put up a good front. Certainly no one could be stauncher than Judith, who, as chief officer for UNHCR's humanitarian efforts in the former Yugoslavia, has ridden into devastated towns in Bosnia in an armored personnel carrier and coolly returned to a firebombed office in Belgrade. Judith, who toured the humid, overcrowded refugee camps of Thailand in the eighties and spent four years in Bangkok working to achieve asylum for Vietnamese boat people. And through long years of practice I have constructed a facade of my own. But it is easy to speak up for civil rights, sit in against the Vietnam War, march for equal rights for women. These issues, in a way, are safely impersonal.

Illness, disability, the specter of permanent damage, on the other hand, are deeply personal, immediate, and terrifying. They call up my adored father, who had never spent a day in bed until his first heart attack. He feared sickness of any sort; I think he felt it bespoke weak character. If as a child I was sick in bed with the flu, measles, or some undiagnosed fever, he would hover in the doorway but never cross the threshold. I took his unease as rejection and it made a stoic out of me.

There is nothing more to do except wait for morning. We don't really discuss my plight, but Judith's empathy surrounds me like an aura. She offers to spend the night in my room, since the other bed is currently vacant. Typically, we find a neutral activity to distract us, last Sunday's Doublecrostic. It would be fun to construct one, we agree. Oh, in another country without pain, another life without uncertainty, to loll about at leisure with a good dictionary and construct a Doublecrostic!

August 26

I travel an hour by ambulance; Judith rides in front with the driver. I lie flat, headfirst, in the back. This helpless position I am in is beginning to feel permanent. The attendant who rides in the back with me takes my vital signs every ten minutes or so and tells me about his childhood as an army brat in Turkey, offering a welcome diversion from my carsickness and fear.

It turns out that the dreaded fluoroscopy is nothing more than a series of moving X rays which the surgeon can watch on a television screen. The slippage is indeed confirmed, but he will reset the bone here and now without resorting to surgery, at least for the time being. With the help of a technician—four hands are required for this intricate maneuver—he unscrews the sidebars of the halo and proceeds to force my neck back into the correct position. It is an exquisitely emotionally painful procedure. I can feel the grinding and clanking of the readjusted bars, the torque wrench fastening on the screws, and the sensation of applied tension. What is happening to my spinal cord, that fragile conduit on which all mobility depends? What if one of my broken displaced vertebrae presses on it, nicks or dislodges it? I have no control over what these mighty men hovering over me are doing. I might as well have my head in a meat grinder.

Because the fluoroscopy pictures are somewhat blurred, the surgeon orders individual X rays as he adjusts my neck. The entire procedure, including five separate adjustments and five sets of films, takes about thirty minutes. I am exhausted. I am in pain from all the manipulations. But because this is an outpatient procedure, no one will offer me any medication.

Now I am cantilevered to the left and my head is tipped downward in this new compensatory position. I complain to the surgeon that I have a vivid view of shoetops and floor tiles and little else. He says airily: "Whatever position we put them in, people in halos get used to it." Before the attendants wheel me out to the ambulance for the trip back to the rehab hospital, I ask what I can do to hasten the healing process. One radiologist suggests envisioning a bird building a nest at the top of my spinal column. A nurse recommends biofeedback. The surgeon merely advises: "Cross your fingers."

August 27

Little by little I've started trying to read. Victor brings me several of the *New Yorker* magazines I have missed and I am able to hold one on my lap on a stack of pillows. Using my left hand, which has a little agility, I turn the pages. At first I can only manage a paragraph, and even that is excruciating as I have to keep shifting my focus and changing the angle at which I hold the page. I am unable to support anything heavier or broader than a magazine. I've always been a galloping reader, racing for information, hurtling past intervening advertisements or cartoons, breathless and fascinated with the language. I don't mean to suggest that I didn't read for style. The level of diction, the indirection, the pace and development of, say, an Alice Munro short story, were delicious to me then. But today I find a change in the way I read and comprehend. Because I can only absorb the language paragraph by paragraph, I find myself making connective leaps from what I read to the world around me, juxtapositions and insights that somehow I failed to make time for in the past.

In the July 27 issue I read with fascinated horror Jon Lee Anderson's "Letter from Liberia." The events of the civil war in Sierra Leone almost pale by comparison with his account of cruelties in neighboring Liberia. He interviews a social worker who laments that the perpetrators are not salvageable. He sees them as "time bombs, psychopaths." One such young man, interviewed by a social worker, confesses that he had been assigned to slit open the bellies of pregnant women. He and others of his faction would bet on the sex of the fetus. Now he suffers from hallucinations in which he sees the faces of his victims coming toward him and in his panic he shouts: "It wasn't only me!"

Sharing these sheltered living quarters with forty-nine other injured Americans flings up in my face, hour by hour, that it isn't only me, it's all of us. It's one world. Healed and healing, failed and failing, the looked-after and the abandoned. It's a lesson we Americans haven't begun to learn.

August 28

This morning I wake and give way (as I frequently do) to a wave of silent tears. I cannot bear to be seen weeping. Everyone thinks I'm so tough; I need to keep up the brave facade. But Judith is due to fly back to her UN post in Geneva on September 6 and I cannot bear to relinquish her. These are not Tennyson's "Tears, idle tears, I know not what they mean." I know exactly. I have become totally dependent on this daughter who fronts for me, who anticipates my needs, tends me and my garden, is optimistic about my recovery, yet realistic about my deficits. I manage to get upright enough to dial our home phone number with an unstable index finger that waggles dangerously between digits. I catch her just before she sets out for her morning walk with the dogs. It is hard for me to ask her to stay on, but when I do so, she says she has lain awake much of the night thinking the same thing. She will extend her leave until September 21. My relief creates a new freshet of tears.

When Judith was nine years old, she went off to spend part of the summer with an old college chum of mine, an hour's drive distant, whom I had recently remet through her husband. He was my very jolly colleague in the English Department at Tufts University, where we were both consigned to teach freshman English classes. He had liberal arts students. I, female, was only entrusted with phys ed majors and dental technicians. Coincidentally, he had been Victor's classmate at Harvard.

Theirs was a very horsey family. My college chum was a superb equestrian; my colleague had learned to ride as a concomitant to the marriage. Each of their children had a horse of his and her own, and there was ample opportunity for Judith to practice serious horsemanship. Every night after supper either we or they placed a phone call. Invariably, as soon as Judith came on the line tears would ensue.

"Joopsie, what's wrong?" I asked the first time. "Don't you like it there? Are you homesick? Do you want us to come get you?"

"No," she sobbed. "I *love* it here. I *love* Bay Lady. We're *cantering*. I just can't stand hearing your voice."

Judith has been an expatriate for nearly thirty years. After a stint as simultaneous interpreter for the European Common Market, she joined the staff of the United Nations High Commission for Refugees, and has held demanding posts in Bangkok and Belgrade as well as serener positions in Bonn and Geneva. Although I am now the one who cries at her departures, I feel certain that she is still conflicted between the home she left and the work she loves. ("We're *cantering*.") Although we exchange daily E-mails and weekly phone calls, it is not the same as having her on this side of the Atlantic.

August 29

I wake to find I have two working heels. Imagine! Toes and heels, even though my right hand still cannot hold a pencil or a fork.

Today is the day for the second attempt at getting me off the Foley catheter. I am dubious and prepared to fail, but one of the more sympathetic aides installs me on the toilet, turns on the shower, and tells me to take all the time I need. "You'll do it," she says. "Just relax and listen to the water."

I close my eyes, imagine water running in Second Brook above our farmhouse, and magically my body reasserts itself. I am finally free of attachments! For a week, though, ever mistrustful, I ask to have the water turned on, and for the rest of my sentient life I promise my body I will pay homage to its autonomy in this simple function I have always taken for granted.

This evening I open the August 24–31 double issue of *The New Yorker* and find my poem, a little ghazal that I wrote for Agha Shahid Ali, who is assembling an anthology of them in English by American poets. I was teaching for a semester in Claremont, California, when Shahid asked me to be part of his project. An enthusiastic fan who is a masseuse at the local health club provided me with twice-weekly professional massages while I was there. By speaking the opening line she inspired the following:

On the Table

I was taught to smooth the aura at the end,
said my masseuse, hands hovering at the end.

Inches above my placid pummelled self
did I feel something floating at the end?

Or is my naked body merely prone
to ectoplasmic vapors to no end?

Many other arthritics have lain here
seeking to roll pain's boulder end on end.

Herbal oils, a CD playing soft
loon calls, wave laps, bird trills now must end.

I rise and dress, restored to lift and bend,
my ethereal wisp invisible at the end.

Ironic that "On the Table" runs now, given my present wounded state, but its appearance is pure coincidence. I love working in form and I love the surprises form can exact: the unexpected metaphor, the chime of meter or rhyme reinforcing the image. The ghazal, though, with its strongly end-stopped couplets and repetitions, is probably the least adaptable of ancient forms to the English language. It wants to flower in Farsi, or in a more mellifluous language than our native tongue. An ancient lyric form employing only one rhyme, it is common to Arabic, Persian, and Turkish literature. Traditionally, the poet is supposed to work his or her own name in at the end, but as an American experimenting with a foreign form, I didn't feel I had to go that far.

Still, I'm delighted to see it on the page. Once in print, a poem acquires an authority and authenticity it lacks squatting there in your notebook. Ironic, too, that my little Persian poetry form appears just in the week of the U.S. Embassy bombings in Nairobi and Dar es Salaam. From my hospital bed I watch the carnage halfway around the world.

August 30

I confess to welcoming the distraction of television. Judith and I watch the evening news, Jim Lehrer first, then, exasperated by the thinness of the program, and the tiresome way it lingers on the Diana-one-year-later story, we switch to Peter Jennings. Alas, the commercial news program is even worse. Nothing on Kosovo, nothing about our own foreign policy blunders, nothing about the war in Sierra Leone, where members of one junta invade a village and by way of terrorizing its occupants hack off the arms of men, women, and children. In a UN magazine I see a photo of a young man who had both arms cut off at the elbow and who laments that he will never be able to use a toilet unaided again. Who grieves for him and the others in northeastern Sierra Leone?

I watch a program on "60 Minutes" about a psychologist in California who conducted an experiment around twenty years ago using college students. He divided them into two groups, one half designated as prisoners in a mock jail of his devising, the other half designated as guards. He videotaped the proceedings, which were to last two weeks. In the dehumanizing that took place, at least four prisoners had to be released after only a few days. The video is vivid and appalling. Upper-middle-class, well-educated, clean-cut young men evolved into sadists. Forbidden to use physical abuse, they ordered solitary confinement, assigned push-ups, withheld food or adequate toileting, and closed their fellow classmates up in closets.

It occurs to me that with only minimal encouragement, under the right circumstances these same guards could learn to hack off the arms of their prisoners. Some of both groups were interviewed ten years later. One guard, who is now a businessman, admitted that he had modeled himself after the brutal overseer in *Cool Hand Luke*, the movie that starred Paul Newman and George Kennedy. He admits that it took him only a day or two to assume the overseer's identity—"I can be a mean sumbitch"—and derive pleasure from it. Dismissive, he does not seem inclined to moral judgment; it all happened long ago.

September 1

What astonishes me about human behavior is its variability. Here we are, just fifty patients being taught to live with our disabilities by one hundred nurses, nutritionists, physical therapists, and assorted others.

This equation tallies with the well-known rule of journalism: one dead in the hometown equals one hundred in Philadelphia equals one thousand in Paris equals ten thousand in India. Is there a gene for perennial do-gooders? Is there a common gene for sadists as well? Why do the staff at the hospital care about us? Where are the hackers?

September 3

The discomfort of the halo seems to increase daily. I am told that this is to be expected, because the pins loosen with time. In the early hours of the morning I ring for an aide to help me turn on my left side—I can't turn onto my right side because of the uncomfortable swelling in my upper right arm. I grab the rails of the bed and pull, and she stuffs one pillow behind my back and a smaller one between my calves, to keep my legs from going numb. I am able to go back to sleep in this position, but the price I pay is an open sore on my scalp above the ear, where the piece that holds the left front halo bar in place digs into my head.

September 4

I have a succession of new roommates. Hospital policy being to match roommates by age and stage, my first four are women in their seventies and eighties. Numbers two, three, and four are snorers who send for their sleeping pills right after dinner and then saw wood continuously throughout the Red Sox game, which I watch, the curtain between our beds drawn, on cable TV.

It was Danny who installed the New England Sports Network cable box on the TV in my room. An aide comes when I call and clicks the switch—impeded by the halo, I can't reach quite high enough to catch hold of it—from A to B and I am able to pass an otherwise totally dreary evening in the familiar company of Nomar and Mo, and the two announcers, Jerry Remy and Sean McDonough, whose voices have by now become those of family members.

My fascination with baseball arose from watching a few games with Danny last season. An armchair warrior, he diagnoses every pitch, perceives every strategy in repositioning outfielders and infielders, reads the coaches' signals and groans over questionable calls: "Watch the replay," he'll say. "He was out by a mile!" His passion for the game is contagious; I go from being mildly interested, emotionally uninvolved, to committed spectator to die-hard fan. Often, Danny comes by and watches part of the game with me. If there is no game, he reads to me from Doris Kearns Goodwin's *Wait Till Next Year*. He holds my cold, lifeless right hand in his big, warm left one.

Roommate number four is an especially proficient snorer. At 1 A.M., helpless with rage, I ring the call bell. The night nurse arrives, stands transfixed for a moment by the decibel level, and announces, "We're moving her."

"You mean tomorrow?"

"No. We're moving her out right now. There's an empty bed across the hall. We'll put her in with another snorer."

Her space remains empty for half a day. A new roommate arrives, but, to my astonishment, I am told that I am to be moved as well.

I am trundled down the hall to the dead end—the opposite end from my old room, where I could overhear every conversation, mostly concerning boyfriends or husbands, that took place at the noisy nurses' station. My new roommate, Nicole, is a very attractive twenty-one-year-old woman who has lost the use of her legs. The prospects for her regaining any feeling at all in them are dim. She is clamped into a hard plastic clamshell brace that covers her entire torso; it must stay in place for three months until her back heals from the very extensive surgery. (Later, she makes a bracelet of the fifty-four staples removed from her incision.) Even though her accident—she fell off a second-story ladder—occurred just four weeks ago, she is agile in her wheelchair. In spite of the ever-present pain she feels, in spite of the grim prognosis she faces, Nicole exudes optimism. That very afternoon she leaves to attend a meeting on kayaking saying, "Now this is a sport I can do."

Judith tells me she learned from the case manager that there had been a heated staff meeting to discuss whether Nicole and I should room together, since although we are both spinal cord injuries, fifty-two years separate us.

September 5

Nicole is spending the night with her husband in the hospital's guest suite; family visits are encouraged. The new night nurse helps me to get ready for bed. Leaving, she closes the door firmly. I hear the latch click shut and am seized with an irrational panic. My ears fill with roaring and shrieking. My side rails are up, I am not strong enough yet to extricate myself from the bed without assistance. Delirious with fear, unable even to breathe, I am trapped. I pound and pound on my call button.

Where did this terror come from? In kindergarten at the Convent of the Sisters of St. Joseph, conveniently next door to the house I grew up in, I was told stories of the martyrdom of nuns. They died in a bizarre array of circumstances, but the story I could never let go of was the tale of the nun who was pressed slowly to death. Faithful to the end, she welcomed it. Nothing seemed more terrible to my five-year-old imagination. Now, death by suffocation, death by squeezing the air out of your lungs, the death I came so close to on July 21 reasserts itself in every even mildly claustrophobic situation I encounter—in the elevator, on an examining table, in a room with the door closed.

Martyrdom, penitence, submission were the lessons I absorbed in parochial school. The public school was a mile away; there was no bussing. Moreover, I could come home for lunch. My parents—minimally obser-vant Jews—thought that I was too young to absorb the tenets of Catholicism. They didn't understand how impressionable I was. A life-size crucifix hung at the end of the classrooms hallway; if I squinted at it hard enough, I could make Jesus writhe, dying for all of us over and over. The lives of the saints also reinforced what I already knew from observing my father's dedication to work: one must be prepared to endure every hardship to be saved. In suffering seek salvation, was the message.

Now, I am a penitent like my darling nun, forced to submit not to death by squeezing, but to carrying my halo on my shoulders, my head cantilevered in a forward position, eye level with everyone's navel. I have no peripheral vision and must turn my entire body to see to the left or the right. Every bodily activity I once took for granted is a difficult hurdle. The so-called shower from the waist down as I perch on the shower bench requires the help of an aide to support the shower wand. Trammelled by the shoulder pieces that hold the halo in place, I cannot reach my own feet. It is exquisite torture to have foreign hands washing between my toes and then invading them further to dry them. An aide also must help me dress and undress. In addition to the size 22 V necks, Judith has sacrificed three of my T-shirts by slitting the shoulder seams wide enough to accommodate the halo frame. Squirming into and out of them, even with assistance, is an ordeal.

September 6

It is Sunday, warm and mild. I take my first excursion out of the hospital in the halo. In the morning one of the physical therapists gives me a lesson in car transfers. The trick is to back up to the seat, brace two hands inside, and lower the head and torso to a forty-five-degree angle before sitting down. In the afternoon Danny comes to get me in his Saab and we drive the eight miles to his house. Danny is selected to transport me because his Saab is four years younger than ours and its shocks are a good deal softer.

Even so, it hurts to ride in a car. Every little pothole translates into a sharp pain in the neck. My back hurts, too. Although I can't turn my head to see cars approaching us at intersections, my pulse races; I am irrationally afraid that we will crash. I'm clutching two pillows on my lap to support my weak arms and fighting down my claustrophobia.

The visit is not an unqualified success. I realize how dependent I am on the wheelchair we left behind at the hospital. Everyone is solicitous, supplying pillows, freeing the couch so I can lie supine, bringing me, in a flat-bottomed orange juice glass I can handle, the first wine I've had since July. It's wonderful to be with Victor and

Judith and Danny and Libby all together instead of having them appear sequentially and all too briefly at the hospital. I realize what an effort it is for them to coordinate their visits, still trying to have somebody present at lunch and at supper to help me eat, bringing homemade comestibles, or vegetarian sandwiches on crusty bread from a nearby café.

I am all too well aware of the disruptions I've caused in everyone's life, even selfishly knowing how much I need those twice-daily visits to preserve what's left of my sanity. I think how terrible it is for the fragile elderly patients in this same rehab hospital who rarely receive a visitor, who are glad to see even the dutiful, bored minister or priest whose job it is to pay the weekly or semimonthly call on the faithful. No wonder their diagnosis is "global failure to thrive." Still, I miss my narrow, ordered existence, my bed that goes up and down, my pain pills, my call button. I see that I'm not ready to rejoin society. But when I come back the staff cluster around and ask, "Did you have a wonderful time?" I realize how impatient they are for me to give the right answer.

September 8

Luckily, Nicole likes baseball too. She is also a vegetarian. We've decided that we are contemporaries, in a sense. I say I am still sixteen years old in the head. We buoy each other through dark periods.

Her two-year-old comes to visit and plays endlessly at unhooking and rehooking the charts at the foot of our beds. She takes him for wheelchair rides on her lap, and after she is back in bed he pushes the empty chair with the skill of a race-car driver. He seems unfazed by her condition, never asking her to pick him up. Her husband stops by on his way home from the auto repair shop where he is a mechanic. He, who is so good at fixing broken transmissions, has a hard time accepting that although her broken back has been reconstructed, her legs are unlikely to work again.

This end of the hall is given over to spinal cord injuries. There are four of us: Nicole and I, and, in the room opposite, two young men, one paraplegic after a diving accident, and the other, Richard, also in a halo. Richard broke two cervical vertebrae, C5 and C6, when his truck rolled over. He had fusion surgery immediately after the crash and shows me the incision on his throat; mine will be performed on the back of the neck at some as yet undetermined future date. He talks with relish of his accident: "When I picked up the deer in my headlights—I think it was a doe because I didn't see any antlers—I thought, Oh no, I can't hit this animal. I swerved to the left, then I overcorrected and overcorrected again. The deer got away but I rolled over three times and landed on the median. I was driving my new Ford pickup. It has jump seats in the cab and I had three passengers. They kicked out the back window and walked away. Incredible. I was the only one hurt."

So far I haven't found a way to talk about my accident at all. I haven't asked anybody who was there to tell me what happened. I haven't had the courage yet to ask people who witnessed the scene to describe it to me. But the moment of truth is coming. The RN at our end of the hall has become a special friend. For one thing, she brings my sleeping medication at ten-thirty and leaves it on my table to take when Nicole's nightly ablutions are completed. This alone is highly irregular. Most nurses stand over you until you swallow the pills lest you secrete them for resale or store them up to take all in one gulp.

We've learned that if you don't get your medications well before the shift changes at 11 P.M., you may have to wait till midnight for someone to arrive. Only RNs are permitted to dole out medications and there are only two RNs on duty at a time. Requests go through an aide and are relayed up the chain of command. The nursing staff leaving and the nurses coming on duty are inundated with duplicate paperwork. If I were the czar of everything, I'd bridge these two shifts somehow so people like Nicole and me, last awake on the floor, don't get trapped in limbo.

But this nurse is quite pragmatic. "I don't worry about *you*," she says. "I know you can't fall asleep in that contraption without it." This night quite casually she asks me exactly what happened on July 21. For the first time I find myself answering. "My horse bolted," I say, and am surprised to burst into tears.

September 9

    Across the way, Richard lies immobilized on his back. He calls the nurse by puffing into a flexible tube that hovers in front of his mouth. My first night here they offered me the same device, but I recoiled in claustrophobia—the same problem I had in the beginning with the omnipresent spoon. If Richard ever feels helpless, he doesn't admit it. Both of us were spinal cord injury patients in the same intensive care unit. But for some reason, he was very lightly medicated while I spent much of that period in a morphine haze.

"I didn't know I could ask for sleeping pills," he told me. "I mean, I'd never been sick, never really been in a hospital before. So I'd just lie awake all night focussing on my legs—I had no feeling at all in them for the longest time. I'd lie there and make myself remember what they used to feel like. It must be something like what yogis do. And then one night I discovered I could twitch this one muscle up here in my right quadriceps. I practiced all night, and the next morning when my doctor came in, I showed him that I could move my big toe."

I'm the only one whose legs can cross the corridor. Nicole says that between her arms and my legs we make a whole person.

We go to bed late because Nicole has to be catheterized before we turn the lights out—her bladder must be emptied every six or seven hours. The nursing staff is teaching her how to do this herself. She is also learning to transfer from bed to wheelchair and back without using the wooden slide board. In the beginning she inched her way from chair to bed and vice versa along this board; many paraplegics never achieve the arm

strength and agility that allow them to dispense with
it. We have started to work out together every night,
wearing our wrist weights. Nicole has to fasten my left
one for me as the fingers of my right hand are not up
to the task of threading strap through buckle. We lie
supine, pumping iron, inning by inning urging the Red
Sox on.

We're very popular here in our room—it's the biggest
on the floor and boasts an alcove not visible from the
doorway. Drop-ins by staff members are frequent. The
Red Sox game is a big draw. There are certain aides and
nurses whose life histories we have heard. More than
half of these women (there is just a handful of male
professionals here) are their families' primary support.
Several have husbands who are disabled or otherwise
unemployable. Everybody has children, and snapshots
substantiate this fact. The petite Filipina RN shows us
pictures of the fattest four-month-old baby I have ever
seen. Somehow she is managing to breast-feed him
while holding down an eight-hour shift. Nicole and I
refer to him as The Whale.

Nurse's aide is a low-paying job; here, only full-
timers are entitled to health benefits, and to keep costs
down the hospital employs a number of "per diems."
Still, there are intangibles that seem to serve as com-

pensation to these women. I learn daily that altruism is alive and well here. More than one aide, helping me brush my teeth, cleaning up a glass of juice I've tipped over, or steadying me as I struggle up from the wheelchair, confesses that she prefers this job to a better paying one in a nursing home because here she gets to see her patients go home. One stands beside me at the mirror this evening and coaxes me to look at my trapped self, then hugs and tickles me to force a smile. I look gaunt and tilted to one side in the cage that encases my head and shoulders, but the same face I remembered looks out at me. My image isn't nearly as grotesque as I had feared.

September 10

One of my physical therapists is practicing a form of relaxation known as Reiki in hopes of achieving some pain relief for me. She puts her hands gently on my face. I flail out in all directions and somehow am able to get upright in my terror. Tears stream down my cheeks. This is not the only time I react to what I perceive as entrapment like a helpless child battling nighttime demons.

My old friend Tim O'Brien, who once wrestled fallen

trees out of our pastures in New Hampshire, confessed recently in an interview with the *New York Times* that in his recurring nightmare the Vietnam War is still going on. Night after night he is drafted again. My own terror began with that first terrible moment when I hit the ground, lost all feeling in arms and legs, and found I could not breathe.

Now seven weeks have elapsed and I am up to learning the details of the first days after my accident. I ask for and receive the discharge summary from the critical care hospital. Reading it, I begin to understand my claustrophobia: "The patient unfortunately had to be intubated in the emergency room because of the development of stridor and the need to protect her airway." Translation: Like my martyred nun, I was suffocating.

I am told the terrors will diminish. I am told to practice deep breathing. But after sunset is still the worst time. Every night I am confronted anew by a mounting sense of dread. I cannot tolerate having the door closed, and cannot sleep with it open. Even with medication, there are nights when sleep evades me. If only, like Ra, I could drop down under the world and begin the slow journey back to sunrise.

September 13

Another Sunday. This time I travel all the way to the farm in Judith's rental car, a modest American vehicle with even softer shocks than Danny's Saab. I am marginally better about oncoming cars and trucks but still flinch at intersections. The twenty-mile trip ends with three miles of rutted dirt road. Every jounce sends a sharp signal across the back of my neck, no matter how I stiffen and brace myself with my hands. I almost cancelled this visit, I am so anxious about exchanging the security of the hospital routine for the hazards of my own home, its narrow staircase and low lintels.

Our farmhouse, a simple twin-chimney post-and-beam Colonial crafted by none-too-skilled carpenters, is two hundred years old. Nothing in it is plumb or true. "All of my doors are held open by stones," I wrote in an early poem. The beautiful wide-board pine floors undulate like the surface of a glossy pond. The attic stringers are made from whole tree trunks, the last of the enormous once-native chestnuts that were wiped out in the blight.

Victor is waiting as we come uphill on our winding, dead-end road. How foreign everything looks! I can hardly believe that I lived here once. The dogs greet me, but not with their usual exuberance, blocking and crowding the car door so that it is difficult to emerge. They hang back just a little, sniffing me and appraising my new situation. Once I am safely settled in the living room they take up their positions guarding me, one on either side. I bury my hands in their fur, a perfect fit. My old life is coming back as I sit absently stroking these warm bodies. I ask myself, how do people live without dogs?

At about four-thirty, the horses stroll in from the back fields and stand patiently waiting in the paddock. I watch from the living room window as Victor goes out to put them in stalls for their evening ration of grain; in a very few minutes he turns them all back out to tackle the widely spaced hay piles he has distributed. Five hay piles await four horses. Although Boomer can't count, she drives each horse in succession away from one pile after another so that it looks like an equine version of musical chairs. No one seems to mind playing this game. She is, after all, the alpha mare and this is the tribute she exacts. Deuter, the only gelding, is always the last to be allowed his own hay, a situation he has come to accept. I love being able to look out almost any window in this house at any season and see our horses. Today they look supremely indolent and content and a little too fat.

The sheep are gone. They came in June as they do every year, four ewes that belong to a weaver friend. Once their annual lambs are weaned, we take this little flock to browse in our rocky sheep pasture just below the house. I consider this their vacation, and they do us a favor, too, keeping this area mowed and fertilized with their little raisin droppings. As the growing season ends they begin to explore and press against the fence-line. The first escape, which invariably takes place at night accompanied by much racing around and baaing, signals it is time to return to their home fold. As a vegetarian, I don't let myself think of their lambs being raised for slaughter.

Before supper I go gingerly up the stairs with their shallow treads and uneven risers, Victor, ever vigilant, behind me. I've had so much "gait training" in the gym and so many sessions doing the hospital's back stairs—up two flights, down two flights, keep your eyes up, look straight ahead, no fair grabbing the handrails—that our twelve steps are an easy ascent, even though the treads were intended for much smaller feet. In our bedroom I lie down on what now seems to me a foreign piece of furniture. It feels softly welcoming. Probably here, I think, I could sleep without a towel roll stuffed under the halo to support the back of my neck, which has been abraded raw by the bleached hospital linens.

Everything is different: no railings on the bed, no grab bars in the bathroom. Mirrors galore, green plants at the windows, framed pictures of the family at various ages. My favorite, enlarged from a snapshot Victor took: Jane, Judith, and Danny, ages five, four, and a year, all lying prone, the girls' heads propped in their hands. Danny, still toothless, blue-eyed and blandly innocent, the much-cosseted small prince, supports himself on his hands between his sisters. Coming back down the stairs, again guarded by Victor, I have to duck to avoid hitting the halo on the overhang.

Supper begins with borscht, a cold soup made from our own beets and onions blended with yogurt (traditionalists use sour cream), and proceeds with what is almost the last of our late corn, slender, white-kerneled Silver Queen that Victor has just fetched from the garden amid dire admonitions not to pick any underripe ears. But I hate the fact that everyone must scurry round to find a chair with a back soft enough to accommodate the hard plastic frame of my halo vest. I hate not being able to butter my own corn. I resent having to limit my wine intake to one glass for fear of jeopardizing my hard-won mobility. I remember dining out with Judith on several occasions in Geneva and a halcyon week we spent together in Paris and how effortlessly we downed a bottle of Bordeaux or Burgundy between us at each evening meal. "Wine is food," we said ritualistically as we clinked glasses.

We turn into the hospital parking lot just as it is getting dark. As we enter this brightly lit, well-ordered place I feel slightly guilty to be comforted by my return. My hospital room has come to feel so much like home that I wonder where I really live.

September 15

In occupational therapy each day I am faced with a bewildering variety of tasks: fitting pegs into holes, extracting pennies from putty, and, today, learning to hold a pen that has been fitted with a foam sleeve to make it easier to grasp. I try to sign my name and am grief-stricken by these huge wobbling letters that were once so carelessly dashed off as I signed personal correspondence, checks, and, after poetry readings, my own books. How will I ever be able to write comments in the margins of my students' poems and stories? How will I even scribble a grocery list?

September 17

Today my elder daughter Jane is getting married in California. Judith has elected to stay at the farm while the rest of the East Coast family flies off to San Francisco. I am genuinely glad that Victor will have a little respite from looking after me and guiltily grateful that Judith chose to stay in his place.

After the accident, Jane and Scott offered to postpone the ceremony till spring but the rest of the family urged them not to. Though I was still too sick to participate in the decision-making, I was glad they agreed to go ahead. The planning had been elaborate and detailed. They had selected the little stone Swedenborgian church, a San Francisco heirloom erected in 1890, no longer in religious use and thus free of Christian symbology.

Although Scott is nominally Unitarian, he wanted a genuinely Jewish ceremony to take place under the canopy known as a chuppah. This cloth cover may be intended to remind worshippers of the forty years the ancient Hebrews spent wandering unprotected in the desert, or perhaps it is a pagan remnant designed to guard the lucky couple from hovering devils. As groom, Scott looked forward to performing the ritual of crushing a glass goblet underfoot, thought by some to signify the destruction of the second temple, by others to ward off evil spirits, and by still others to symbolize the rupturing of the bride's hymen. But to consummate this religious ceremony required finding a rabbi willing to perform a mixed marriage in what had at least at one time been a church. Myriad telephone calls and conferences, many referrals, hopes raised and then dashed. It was likely Jane and Scott would have to settle for a secular service performed by a justice of the peace. At the eleventh hour, a rabbi who moonlights as a rabbi—he has another full-time job—agreed to join these two middle-aged lovers in holy matrimony.

A month later, on a video of the event, I see what sort of rabbi they so serendipitously found. Earthy, pragmatic, humorous yet properly spiritual, he delivered a simple and nondogmatic homily.

To Scott, he said, "Don't flirt. Don't fight the fight you've already won or the fight you've already lost. Learn how to apologize. You're a leader; be a model to others. And be romantic. Send your wife flowers. Buy her expensive jewelry." (This last remark brought the house down.)

To Jane: "Make sure your house is a home. Be a matchmaker; remember your single friends. Remember that Scott is your main man."

To the newlyweds together: "And remember, religion never made a bad marriage good or a good marriage bad."

I, who am allergic to men of the cloth no matter what pattern it is cut from, found this rabbi to be charming.

Jane, who always projects an air of quiet dignity, wore a mid-calf white dress sequinned with seed pearls. The luster from these highlighted her silver hair, stunningly gray since her thirties. Music was provided by a cellist friend. The four poles of the chuppah were supported by Danny, Danny's son, Scott's brother, and Scott's brother's son, thus providing perfect familial symmetry.

Immediately after the ceremony, the bride and groom call me on their cell phone. From my hospital room I am connected with the revelry three thousand miles away.

"Hello, Max?" Scott's big confident voice booms in at me from a San Francisco sidewalk. "I just married your daughter, it's all signed and sealed."

Then Jane's voice. "Mom? We miss you, Mom. It was wonderful."

I look around me. Wheelchair, paper cups, pills, a bedside tray. The tap of crutches going past my open door. What can I say back to such immediate happiness?

Later, Victor calls to report on the wedding dinner.

Of course he made a toast, but Danny's eight-year-old son Noah stole the show with a toast of his own, repeating a telephone conversation he had overheard between Jane and me a few days before the big event. My poised and quietly self-assured older daughter was having second thoughts.

"Everybody gets prewedding jitters, Janeo," I said. "I'll never forget just before I went down the aisle. Suddenly I thought, I'm making a terrible mistake! I turned to my father and said: 'What am I doing here? I'm not even sure I want to marry this man!' My father gave me his arm and said: 'Just pretend it's a rehearsal.'"

It has been, as Victor likes to say, a marriage for life. It is hard to accept that we now belong to the elderly population, but statistically this is true. We have joined the "oldbodies" of our culture, an affectionate term I was introduced to by my poet friend William Meredith. There's a lot to be said for the continuity of a long marriage. I am not speaking of the fuzzy companionship, feet up on the fender of the woodstove, but of the deep unspoken intimacy that develops when you have raised a family together in suburban Boston, naively bought a derelict farm, invested thirty-five years of hard labor in the property, filled the empty nest with dogs and horses and sheep and cats, and watched the seasons, suburban and rural, inexorably give way to one another for over fifty years.

Once we were young and poor and passionate. We lit out like Huck for the territory, turning our backs on the rigid family structures we had both left behind. Victor's mother was widowed when he was only five. Surviving the Depression absorbed most of her energy; there wasn't much money left over for luxuries. Certainly none for sports equipment. Mostly, Victor hung out with other boys from the neighborhood, playing a kind of street baseball with sticks and a tennis ball.

One day last year we observed a pack of small boys jumping their bikes over the inert form of a little girl they had persuaded to lie at the bottom of a driveway and Victor intervened, demanding they abandon this sport.

As we walked on, I said, "Well, kids that age think they're immortal. Didn't you have a bike as a kid?"

"My brother had a bike. We were supposed to share it. And then it got stolen." He said this without bitterness and without further amplification.

I grew up in the sort of authoritarian household in which children were to be seen and not heard. My father, a pawnbroker, left the house at six-thirty each morning and returned after six at night, except for Saturdays when he worked until 10 P.M. When he was present, his word was law and his right the divine right of kings. As little as I knew him, I worshipped at his throne. What I lightheartedly refer to as my Jewish Calvinist work ethic—salvation through grace and grace through hard work—came down to me in a direct line of descent. I can still hear my father sigh, at the close of a Sunday during which he had read the entire *New York Times*, taken a brief walk, and dozed in his Barca-Lounger: "Well, I murdered this day."

My mother sat on her own pedestal, ordering the groceries by phone, going into the city to shop for clothes or to meet a friend for lunch. Her social service was limited to reading to the blind, which usurped one afternoon a week. After three sons, she longed for a daughter to dress up and display, a role I fiercely resisted. The rift between us grew as deep as the Grand Canyon.

Looking back, I regret that I disappointed my mother so profoundly and for so long. She wasn't happy about my early marriage, our three stair-step children, and she was appalled when we bought the farm. She had grown up in rural Virginia, the sixth child of the proprietor of the general store, followed by six more siblings. They were the only Jewish family in town. At eighteen, she had escaped to the bright lights of Philadelphia; she took our defection to the country as a deliberate disloyalty. But we reconciled our differences in time, and our children brought her enormous pleasure as she grew older. As I said about the two of us in a sonnet sequence, "We both agreed that what I'd birthed was good."

Victor and I wanted something very different for ourselves and for our children: a rapport between parents and their offspring that we had never enjoyed. In the blissful ignorance of our twenties we had three children within five years. Willy-nilly, we all grew up together.

One of the chief and sustained pleasures of our old age is that we have all stayed on very good terms with one another. Somehow we've managed to narrow the generation gap to a workable aperture. Very little is held back on either side. Frequently, though, we find out from one adult child what is going on in the others' lives, and we know that they are calling across continents to find out what we are doing. If anyone is the sinner who spreads the family linen abroad to air, I confess to the charge. "Don't tell her anything," they say of me, rolling their eyes in mock horror. "She'll put it in a poem. She'll make it up, she'll change it around, but she'll put it in a poem."

In 1996, when Victor and I had been married for fifty years, I wrote this poem:

The Long Marriage

The sweet jazz
of their college days
spools over them
where they lie
on the dark lake
of night growing
old unevenly:
the sexual thrill
of PeeWee Russell's
clarinet; Jack
Teagarden's trombone
half syrup, half
sobbing slide;
Erroll Garner's
rusty hum-along
over the ivories;
and Glenn Miller's
plane going down

before sleep
repossesses them . . .

Torschlusspanik.
Of course
the Germans have
a word for it,
the shutting of
the door,
the bowels' terror
that one will go
before
the other as
the clattering horse-
hooves near.

So much is taken for granted in a good relationship, whether among family members or between humans and their animals. Victor and his mare Boomer know each other so well that each can read the other's thoughts. I see Boomer standing passively as Victor prepares to mount. He is telling her, indeed beseeching her, "Whoa, now, whoa," and she is thinking, No way I'm going to whoa. You've got your leg over, haven't you? And she sets off downhill, comfortable with their compromise.

But if he were to shift his weight, jump or fall off, she would stop immediately and wait for him.

On the hundred-mile competitive trail rides, the rider comes into the first vet check at twenty miles out. His horse must pass pulse, respiration, and dehydration tests in order to continue. He may have only ten minutes to cool his horse out and prepare for the vet's evaluation. It would be useful if his animal would urinate now, during this rest period. Victor leads Boomer over to the tall grass, opens his fly, and pees. She then pees companionably along with him.

Elizabeth Bishop's translation from the Portuguese of Vinícius de Moraes's "Sonnet of Intimacy" hung on the corkboard over my desk for more than a year before it got displaced by some other poem. In it Moraes describes farm afternoons when "there's much too much blue air." Here is Bishop's rendition of the last six lines:

> The smell of cow manure is delicious.
> The cattle look at me unenviously
> and when there comes a sudden stream and hiss
>
> Accompanied by a look not unmalicious,
> All of us, animals, unemotionally
> Partake together of a pleasant piss.

Who but Bishop could capture this seemingly art-
less simplicity and earthiness in exacting iambic pen-
tameter? This, with its apt and yet unexpected rhymes,
is one worth storing in the memory bank.

September 19

It's a Saturday. The rest of the family is attend-
ing Jane's post-wedding party in Napa. Judith comes
to take me home for the day, a laborious trip with my
standard two pillows. I brace myself as we pass over
the dirt roads.

All this week I've been practicing doing grassy
knolls and pebble-strewn mounds with my physical
therapist, preparing to climb the hill to my garden and
our pond. Despite the halo, I am determined to con-
quer the steep grade and visit my vegetables. The path
is thickly strewn with shagbark hickory nuts that roll
underfoot like marbles. There is a short delay while these
are raked away.

Judith has enlisted the help of a friend to walk up
the hill with us, carrying a lawn chair lest I need to sit
down. An unnecessary precaution; I am in better shape
than either of them realizes. All those grueling walks

around the periphery of the hospital, plus all my workouts on the gym's various leg and hip machines, have paid off.

Given the time of year, the garden is still flourishing. Spinach, radishes and corn have gone by, but the brassicas—cabbage, broccoli, cauliflower—are still thriving. So are the yellow pattypan squash and the zucchini that Victor won't touch. There is the usual glut of mostly green tomatoes. We make our way to the little sandy beach fifty yards distant. I sit gratefully in a lawn chair to watch Victor's brook trout leaping for insects and enjoy the last red dragonflies hovering over the surface of the water.

Shortly after we arranged with the state conservation service to convert the original marsh on this site to a spring-fed pond, I wrote the opening stanza of my poem "We Are," a poem my daughter-in-law read in my place at Jane and Scott's wedding:

> Love, we are a small pond.
> In us yellow frogs take the sun.
> Their legs hang down. Their thighs open.
> On our skin waterbugs suggest incision
> but leave no marks of their strokes.
> Touching is like that. And what touch evokes.

In my life before the accident, I climbed up and down this hill many times a day, to and from the garden, the pond, and the driving dressage ring that lies just beyond. Today I am exhausted. Did I ever expect to get back here?

Although it is under an acre in size, the pond is hugely significant for us. We water the garden from it. Deer and other woodland creatures drink here; great blue herons come to pilfer Victor's trout. Wild ducks— mallards, mergansers, even little wood ducks—come and go in their migrations. In winter, before the first snow, we skate on its icy surface.

Surrounded by pine and hemlock, the pond fits so naturally into the landscape that no one can believe it is man-made. Years ago we installed, shovelful by shovelful, a little sandy beach by the diving rock, and after that Victor and I made a pact. We agreed to take an hour every afternoon just to sit and enjoy our little pond kingdom. Every good summer day, we swam, skinny dipping among the trout and turtles. When we had guests we offered them the option to join us au naturel.

Before we return to the rehab hospital, Judith and I make a trip to the barn. I can't duck between the fence boards in my usual fashion because of the halo, but Judith unlatches the gate and, a bag of carrots at the ready, we cross the paddock to the stalls. Boomer's older daughter, Praise, clearly recognizes me and is mildly intrigued by my headgear. Boom's Hallelujah (Lu) has eyes only for the carrots, as does her mother. But Deuter takes one look at my bird cage, snorts his fear snort, and retreats to the back of the stall. He is unwilling to approach me but flicks an ear in response to my voice.

We stand around for quite a while, feeding carrot bits to the others, but my own best-loved horse will not come up to me. I'm not steady enough to slide the latch and go in to greet him up close, but I am not deeply disappointed. I've lived with this horse for seventeen years and I know the depth of Deuter's aversion to new stimuli. Year after year he reacts with terror to snow melting and slipping off the barn roof. The others, too, kick up their heels and race out to the back pasture when a sheet of snow comes avalanching off the barn overhang, but it's a rollicking game for them, and they soon race back in. Not Deuter. He will hang back in the field all day until one of us goes out with halter and lead rope and soothing words to bring him in.

And yet, he has always been a pleasure when it comes to what the British call "putting to"; he stands calmly while the cart or sleigh is pulled up behind him, the shafts are slipped into the tugs, the breeching and overgirth straps are fastened, adjusted, readjusted. Perhaps he takes some comfort from the feel of the shafts along his sides enclosing him, the way our dogs take comfort in denning up in the corner of a room behind a chair.

He has never given the farrier a problem, even when hot shod, a process in which the heated metal shoe is sear-fastened to the hoof, with resultant smoke and smell. He is not brave about the annual inoculations, but many horses react like small children to the sight of the syringe and needle. Under saddle he is a true gentleman, stands stock still to be mounted and does not move off until asked. He is responsive to every cue of legs, seat and hands, and he has a comprehension of about ten verbal commands, including "wait" and "okay." All our horses come when called because they know there is probably a treat lurking in the human's hand, but Deuter *answers*. His neigh is a distinctive gravelly bass.

And so, even though he is too spooked to come to me today, it's almost enough to see him in the safety of his home environment. I know some people have had a horse put down after such an event because they could not bear to look at him again. Do I forgive Deuter for having almost killed me? Do I love him any less? I forgive him for doing what he could not help doing;

there was no malice in his bolting. My affection for him is unchanged and I am confident that so is his for me.

September 20

Victor, Danny, and his family return from California with a hundred candid snapshots of everything and everybody except the actual ceremony, from which amateur cameras were banned. (Professional stills are to come.) I'm pleased that Victor had a little time away from his problematic wife but grieve that Judith must leave tomorrow.

September 21

This evening Judith flies back to Geneva. A family meeting is scheduled at the rehab hospital for noontime to plan for my discharge. Each of my therapists comes, makes a brief report, and goes. The atmosphere is one of mutual congratulation; everyone says what a wonderful job everyone else has done. It is predicted that I will manage well back in my home environment. I sit silent during this tableau. The main cautionary directive is that someone should precede me going downstairs so as to cushion my spine in case I fall, and walk behind me when I climb stairs in case I tip over backward. With the halo on, weighting me forward, I am more vulnerable to falling on my face; my PT says I will automatically catch myself on my hands. I try to believe this.

It is very hard to say goodbye to Judith. Nicole, whether through tact or by happenstance, manages to absent herself as we say our farewells, quite teary on my part. I can't be too sad, knowing Judith plans to return as soon as we have a date for the surgery that everyone anticipates I will undergo in late October.

Tomorrow, Richard goes back to the primary care hospital to have his halo removed, a consummation I long for. He promises to tell me every step in the procedure, even though I am probably a month away from being liberated. (So much for the early elastic sentence of eight to twelve weeks—I am to serve out the full term.) Nicole decrees that we will have a party to celebrate Richard's release from the diabolical head constraint. Since friends have brought her the first pickings from a nearby apple orchard, she decides we will make an apple pie. I am dubious about my contribution to this venture.

Nicole trundles off in her wheelchair to wheedle all the necessary ingredients from the hospital kitchen.

We agree to assemble the pie in our room so as not to miss the Red Sox game. Peeling is a disaster. I am quite simply unable to operate any of the three vegetable peelers extant—two of them from the guest suite kitchen on our floor. However, I am able to cut the shortening into the flour using two plastic knives, then add the water and knead the dough with my hands. This cheers me up a little. Anything I can do with my hands counts as occupational therapy.

Nicole takes over peeling the apples, then cores and slices them on her freshly washed slide board. We roll the crust out on the hospital-room desktop. She manages to fit it into the pan. After the top crust is on, I flute the edges with my weaker hand, and find it easier than the Thera-Putty.

September 22

Richard, halo-less, wheels into our room.

"It was a piece of cake," he says. His doctor loosened the bars and lifted all four pins away from his head with one deft upward move.

"My God! Look at you! Look how you have a top to your head. And hair!" I say. "How does it feel?"

"About twenty pounds lighter." Even though he is

now in a high plastic collar, he's able to move his neck a few degrees from side to side. "Big improvement in visibility, too."

The marks from his forehead pins glisten bright red. "Richard, what about those stab wounds?"

"The doc says to swab 'em out twice a day with a Q-Tip. That way I won't get any adhesions."

I'm horrified. The prospect of sticking Q-Tips into my flesh twice a day somehow equates with every other bodily invasion I've suffered over the last two months. "Gross! One more charming ritual," I say.

Richard laughs. "Listen. This is small change compared to what we've been through. You'll see." We're both silent, thinking about my surgery to come.

The party is held in the little alcove off our room. Richard's wife, Ann, arrives for the occasion with shrimp, cheese and crackers, peanuts, and wine. My first roommate unexpectedly drops in, without her walker. She's using a very sporty-looking cane, which she hooks over the bed rail.

Danny arrives soon after, followed by Nicole's husband. They take up the subject of cars. I hear *torque, transmission, fuel injection,* and little spurts of laughter as each outdoes the other with a tale of mechanical woe.

Ann teaches high school English in northern Vermont. Juggling her classes and the three-hour drive each way to spend time with Richard has been—she searches for a neutral word—eventful. Words are our business. We discover that we share a pet peeve.

"Next year the difference between *lie* and *lay* is going to be declared obsolete," I say. "There'll be an act of Congress."

"I know. When I was scouting around rehab hospitals for Richard and came here for a visit, I thought we couldn't bear to stay."

"You mean the way the aides all say 'Now I want you to lay down here?' The doctors say it, too. I know Ph.D.'s who tell their dogs, lay down."

"Lie, lay, lain," Ann recites. In unison we say, "Lay, laid, laid."

The wine goes around. The party becomes very merry. The pie is beatified with praise.

Richard has decided to stay in rehab for another two or three weeks. Although he is still mainly in a wheelchair, by wearing a brace on one ankle he is able to walk considerable distances with a therapist at his side. Every day Richard increases the distance he travels on two feet, which inspires me to work even harder at getting

fit. He entered this hospital with a diagnosis of quadri-
plegia. He is determined to walk out of it. (Although I
am not present for this epiphany, Nicole is. She tells me
later that the little crowd of onlookers cheered as Richard
exited on his own two feet. We don't discuss how this
made her feel about her situation.)

III

September 24

~~~~~ Homecoming day! Victor comes to collect me. The PTs and OTs see us out, along with my case manager and assorted well-wishers, even knowing I will be back in five days to begin outpatient therapy. I try to keep up a good front; I am supposed to be overjoyed, elated, at returning to my native heath, but in truth I am full of foreboding. They are kicking me out of the nest. Now I must go back into the world, still trammelled by this ever more oppressive halo, and try to resume my old life.

Judith has left a variety of prepared meals that need only to be moved from freezer to microwave, and in short order Victor serves up a sumptuous meal. I am unable to eat most of it but I try to share his enthusiasm. My fatigue is overwhelming. (Fatigue, in fact, is my chief complaint for the next several weeks. I am so consistently tired that I begin to fantasize other ailments— leukemia, an undiscovered cancer, a blocked artery.) It seems that I am always in the process of lying down or struggling up to find some more comfortable place to stretch out in—a sofa, a studio couch, the double bed in the little back bedroom. I am grateful for the prescriptions for Restoril and Xanax that came home with me. These have been my nightly mainstays for the last two months, easing me to sleep inside my cage in a fixed position on my back. Even so, I rarely manage more than five hours of unconsciousness on any given night.

September 25

The Visiting Nurse Association sends an RN to check me out at home. A great flurry of taking my vital signs ensues but there is little else for her to do. I have been "rolled over" into VNA care and will be rolled over again in four days into outpatient status. The bureaucracy requires much redundant paperwork. Meanwhile, Victor and I agree to attack my fatigue with daily walks, which we will lengthen a little at a time. These are the halcyon days of a New England autumn. I am sick with nostalgia for the times when we used to forage on horseback for mushrooms, ambling through the now insect-free woods, checking out dead trees for oyster mushrooms and sulphur polypores, and eyeing the ground ahead for other gifts—honey mushrooms, giant puffballs, and sometimes in open fields a crop of meadow mushrooms. My mood is so dour that I almost wish for a dark, rainy day.

September 29

This afternoon we go back to the rehab hospital for my first session as an outpatient. The minute I walk in I am grateful that I made the decision to come here twice a week rather than have a therapist come to the house. Here are the same patients I waved goodbye to last week: Nicole in her wheelchair, other friends in their walkers or on crutches or at the standing table—my people, a small city of cripples to which I belong. I get a warm welcome from the PTs and OTs as well.

Wendy puts me through the usual routine on leg machines, a safe regimen of reclining bicycle, stair step machine, hip machine and lift-the-bar, the one exercise I hate. I can only lift fifteen pounds. Wendy demonstrates that she can raise seventy-five. She says that at this point I am a wimp. I am more amused than offended by her outspoken diagnosis, even though I've always prided myself on staying fit.

We plan to increase the time and tension on each

of these machines little by little. Lastly and best of all, I get to lie on a heat pack while she stretches my quadriceps and adductors. I am wise now in the nomenclature of muscles I had no previous knowledge of. My legs persist in feeling strange, as if newly attached with their wrappings still in place, but as Victor drives me home I feel shriven by my exertions.

October 1

Therapy again today, OT for an hour, followed by PT. I have been faithfully working out every evening with dumbbell weights, having memorized the six exercises given me, and am gradually increasing my range on the right side. In fact, I call Nicole every night at eight to ensure that we are still working out together. (We are to continue this contact for weeks and weeks, long after she too has returned home.)

My outpatient therapist works my arms as I lie on the mat and tries to determine where I am "stuck." Where the carriage ran over my arm there are large nodules under the skin that have not dissolved. These torn muscles keep me from moving freely through the half circle a healthy arm can describe. We then proceed to fine motor exercises, again involving the despised Thera-

Putty and the nasty little pegs that she buries in it for me to extract. There is also a large plastic bowl of rice in which are submerged various small objects: buttons, pennies, the selfsame little pegs, and so on. I am exhorted to remove as many as I can find with an eyebrow tweezer. Finally I am rewarded with a hand massage. She presses the edema out of my fingertips down into my palms to stimulate my circulation, but I have little faith that these simple ploys are going to restart the blood flow. I detest my half-dead hand.

On the home front, my inability to use the computer keyboard without making thousands of errors depresses me. A serendipitous stroke of luck just when I need it. Debbie Brown, a local poet friend on sabbatical from teaching her university courses, is willing to barter critique of her poetry for typing and filing. She warns me that she is a lousy typist and has no office skills, but in truth she moves mountains in my disorderly study. She installs hanging files, which I have never had, then alphabetizes them, an innovation that never occurred to me. She would like to pull out my top middle desk drawer (full of stamps, staples, paper clips, old snapshots, expired membership cards, and obsolete addresses) and debride it. She gently suggests a total rearrangement of available space so as to provide more countertop and less clutter. As is, the computer table is under the window overlooking the paddock. Behind it looms a massive office desk I have had for forty years. Because this is an ancient house and all the floors are atilt, in order to hold myself in place at the computer table, I must reach behind and pull the middle desk drawer out to serve as a brace against the back of the chair. Somehow I have managed to write a book or two in this untenable position, but I do agree. Big changes are in order.

Victor is studying office furniture catalogs. He is going to redo my study to utilize the L-shaped corner and do away with the great lump of desk usurping much of the floor space. The engineer in him wields tape measures and levels. I will have two files, several drawers, a Formica desk surface. He has consulted a local carpenter to install the one-piece top.

October 3

Just yesterday, daughter Jane and her husband arrived on the East Coast; today they come for a visit. Scott is going to prepare dinner tonight and he begins at 4 P.M., in a grandly ebullient style that turns the kitchen into a chef's domain. Jane and my daughter-in-law Libby are the sous-chefs, fetching, mincing, and polishing. We begin with champagne to toast the newly-weds, an elegant hors d'oeuvre of lobster with herbs on melba rounds, and at about 8 P.M. proceed to the main course: grilled fish accompanied by a ratatouille that Scott has assembled from the gifts of my garden. It's a wonderful medley of onions, potatoes, carrots, parsnips, tomatoes, eggplant, and garlic, drizzled with olive oil and roasted in a hot oven. But I am so exhausted by this time that I can't stay up any longer. An hour or two upright at a stretch is as much as I can manage before pain and exhaustion drive me to despair. On Monday Jane and Scott fly off to Paris and Switzerland for a two-week honeymoon. Lucky baby-boomer professionals, who can afford such luxuries!

October 6

    The issue of visitors comes up again, as it did intermittently while I was hospitalized. I don't want any, really. In my early, most vulnerable weeks I fiercely resisted all "compassion-junkies," a useful term I borrow from Robert McCrum's book about recovery from his stroke, *My Year Off*. Today, however, an old friend, Annette Jaffee, is arriving from Pennsylvania for three days. More than twenty years ago, Annette was my student at Princeton, where I taught a creative writing class open to returning adults as well as the usual undergraduates. Four novels later, she is my peer and ally, one of the few outsiders I feel comfortable hosting. Of course I am not hosting; I am the patient and she provides succor, housekeeping, cooking, and congenial conversation for Victor.

Last month, when everyone but Judith flew out to California, I welcomed the support of another old friend, who is now a lawyer but who lived with us one year on the farm when she was trying to make a life decision after college. We've had a succession of bright young women who stayed for a year of mucking out and foal-watching as the mares' due dates drew near. In every instance, they left to finish college, go to law school or get a master's degree, or marry and raise a family. Most of them have stayed in touch. This one, Suzy Colt, left New England for law school in the Midwest but came back to New Hampshire, where she is now in private practice.

In her early years of practice she became quite a celebrity by successfully representing a battered wife who killed her husband in self-defense. I remember sitting at my breakfast table with its view of the paddock she used to muck out and seeing Suzy in her city clothes on the "Today" show. One of the ironies of our country life has been that as we withdrew from the liberal urban activism of the sixties, we propelled a succession of young women who had been in retreat for a variety of reasons to law school, vet school, and the business world.

In the early days of my hospital stay, Suzy filled in for Judith or Victor at noontime, helped me drink my high-energy milk shake, and watched neutrally as I struggled to raise a quarter of a sandwich to my mouth. She smuggled in tiny bottles of Cointreau and Kahlúa to flavor my twice-a-day odious high protein drinks. Since I've been home, she has visited a few times, creating great diversions with the dogs and helping out in the barn, where she is very much at home. (Somehow, the people I could not bear to see were fellow writers and professional associates to whom I presented the status of a fallen warrior, a blinded Oedipus of the other gender. I could only tolerate appearing wounded and helpless to those who didn't value me for my achievements. Sympathy turned me off. Sometimes it reduced me to tears. To be a convalescent is to be in extremis; to visit the convalescent, unless you are a family member or a closely held friend, threatens to tip the balance.)

October 10

I tie my own shoes for the first time. The average four-year-old has somewhat more dexterity than I. Still, I've made the loop with my right hand and poked the other loop through with my left and finally, after several tries, caught it with my sensationless thumb and forefinger and achieved a lopsided bow. "No cheerleading, please," I say to Victor, who oversees this project. He understands the mixture of triumph and shame I feel.

October 11

Victor and I drive up the mountain road to check out a place where we might board the young mares for the winter. We agree that looking after four horses through snow season is too much for one person to deal with. This is a newly renovated equestrian facility in a landscape that is very familiar to us. Two barns, spacious paddocks, fields with run-in sheds, a renovated farmhouse sit atop a plateau of forty acres. Since there is an indoor arena, Praise and Lu can continue to be worked throughout the winter.

The stable has gone through a succession of owners

and is now in the hands of a young woman whose horse-keeping standards are almost as impeccable as mine. (I am a fanatic horsekeeper. Not only are stalls and paddock to be picked out morning and night; the pastures too undergo manure removal several times a week.)

In the sixties, when Judith was an avid pony clubber, the district commissioner of the local pony club lived here. The house was comfortably ramshackle in those days. Dogs of every description went in and out at will. The commissioner found suitable ponies—size-wise, anyway; some were roughcut, green broke critters that she helped shape up—for every kid in town who wanted to join and who would live up to her demands in terms of care.

Coming back here is a nostalgic journey. I still have photos of Judith flying over fences on Dusty, her Arab/Welsh pony, one of a pair we bought at a horse auction one wintry February day when she was twelve. These dapple grays were nicely made, though a little on the thin side. We only wanted one pony, but they were for sale as a pair, as neither had ever been out of the pasture they were housed in without his brother. The Maine farmer who owned them had acquired them in trade for a tractor a year ago, but his adolescent sons preferred car engines to real horsepower. We paid $330 for them both, a very different dollar in the sixties. When Judith went away to college, we sold the ponies, again as a pair, to a wealthy contractor for his only daughter. He, too, made a verbal promise to keep them together and we followed their progress in the show world for several years to come.

My own obsession with equines took root at a very young age. When I was four or five, I was taken to Valley Green, part of Fairmount Park in suburban Philadelphia, where my parents were riding livery-stable horses. Someone boosted me up to sit in front of my father on his horse, which was redolent of sweat. I pressed my palms against its damp neck and my senses took in not only the smell, the feel, of horse but the totality of the unspoken union between horse and human. I have been tracking the course of this union ever since.

October 12

Today marks the end of my twelfth week in the halo. We go back to the hospital to see the surgeon. It is a big fizzle of a day, a total disappointment. The secretary to the orthopedic surgeon seems to have blocked our every effort to reach him by phone to find out what to expect; in the end it turns out that nothing has been scheduled except for a routine vertical cervical X ray. This is, as usual, enigmatic. Perhaps that dark shadow is an unhealed fracture line. Perhaps, since this is merely a two-dimensional view, it is only a shadow. He will have his secretary arrange for a CT scan within two weeks, and after that he will "pencil me in" for surgery.

"Within two weeks!" I say. "But it's been twelve weeks. You said you didn't believe in leaving halos on any longer than twelve weeks."

"The longer it stays on, the better the chances are for healing."

I am furious but manage to keep some composure. "Is there any reason the CT scan couldn't have been scheduled for the same day as the X ray?"

No, he supposes not. It just wasn't.

I tell him that we tried twice to get him to return our calls. I tell him that my case manager at the rehab hospital tried repeatedly to reach him through his secretary to set up an appointment. She told him that his frequent calls were the problem—that was why he hadn't heard back from the surgeon.

"I don't know anything about that," he says.

I sigh. This subject is obviously not worth pursuing; he is above the fray. There is nothing to be gained by pointing out that we must travel an hour each way and that part of our route traverses corduroy dirt roads, which are excruciating in the halo, no matter how I brace myself with pillows.

I tell him the halo feels loose.

"Where?"

"Right hind," I say.

He leaves the room to get his torque wrench and tightens the right rear pin, which of course pulls against the opposing forehead pin. The turn of the screw, I say to myself. I am beginning to hate this man who seems so detached from the process. (In retrospect, I understand that we are both at our battle stations. He is defending my spine against trauma that might destroy its incipient natural healing. I am defending my psyche against having to suffer further incursions while my vertebrae may—or may not—be fusing on their own.)

"After the surgery," I ask, "will I be in a collar or back in the halo?"

"Halo," he replies.

This was the answer I dreaded. (It had been vaguely hinted at in the rehab hospital when I'd quiz an RN or aide who had looked after other spinal fusion cases. No one had actually told me that post-surgicals had to be in halos as opposed to collars, and so I'd believed what I wanted to believe.)

"How long?"

"Four to six weeks."

Oh God, I think, fighting back tears. How can I get through another four to six weeks in this torture device?

October 13

The secretary calls to establish an appointment for a CT scan and fluoroscopy on October 21. Moreover, I am pencilled in for surgery on October 26. Something got through to him after all.

October 14

Victor and I call Judith to tell her about the date for surgery. She will come, she says, in plenty of time; in fact, she will have her secretary check out availability on Swissair flights today. I am in a holding pattern. Victor and I walk every day so that I can stay in shape for the ordeal to come. I continue to go to out-patient therapy twice a week. I see Nicole each of those afternoons and we keep each other's spirits up. Now that she too has been discharged, the rehab hospital van picks her up several mornings a week and brings her to the gym to continue her therapy. Right now, she says, she's in a holding pattern too. Her husband's employers are going to provide a car with hand controls, and that will make a huge difference.

"Once I have wheels, I'll come to see you," she promises.

I, who am conveyed everywhere by husband or son or friend, try to imagine Nicole's isolation. Her little boy is in day care. Her parents and her parents-in-law all have demanding jobs. One of the best mechanics in the business, her husband keeps long hours. Days pass when she sees no one between 8 A.M. and 5 P.M.

"I read a lot," she says. "I'm reading everything I can get my hands on about spinal cord injuries and experiments on nerve regeneration."

"What about school?"

Nicole had been accepted into a graduate program in Boston; she planned to get a degree in social work. I've been lobbying for law school, her second choice.

"Next year," she says. "They're deferring my admission. Don't worry; I'm going to go through with it."

We both miss Richard. I am nostalgic for catching and throwing the beach ball with him under the watchful eye of our two PTs, standing by to catch us in case we fell over. Richard was in the greater danger, as he was precariously upright at that point, but his aim was better than mine, which evened the playing field. By phone he tells me that he is getting around his own house sans wheelchair and uses it mostly to take the dog for a walk. He has someone drive him to the site of the mall his construction firm is building so that he can check on progress. He bothers his wife Ann in the evening while she is grading stacks of high school English papers. We are going to plan a reunion at our farm as soon as the situation is stable.

October 19

The mares are leaving today. Victor hooks up the truck and trailer and with a helper loads Praise and Lu for the short drive across town. I hate seeing them go. I have vivid memories of each of their births, the balletic leaps and plunges of their halcyon first years, the steady care and training involved in bringing them along as reliable horses under saddle and in harness. Even though I know it's a wise course, to have to ship them off to foster care now breaks my heart.

Over the years, my own children repeatedly teased me about caring more for the horses than for humans. "Animals first" became a well-worn family joke. "We're just human beans," they said. But in truth, horses didn't reenter my life until we bought our derelict property in 1963 and made friends with a couple who owned a casual horse farm nearby. Judith promptly became one of the young girls who moved in with them for the summer. Soon she was spending weekends and school vacations there as well. My own enthusiasm was rekindled and from then on there was no turning back.

Those first few years before we had renovated our farmhouse and ancient dairy barn, we leased a succession of mild-mannered school horses from their facility, housing them summers in a run-in area under the sagging barn. Once we were year-round citizens, Victor set about redesigning and restoring this space, a former cow manure pit, to contain six box stalls and an open surface we refer to as the motel lobby. We took riding lessons. I studied veterinary texts and dressage handbooks. On horseback Victor and I explored every footpath in the hills around us until we knew every back route to the next town, and where every one-room schoolhouse had once stood.

It's hilly, unfriendly terrain, full of granite outcroppings, but Arabians are famously surefooted. It seemed to me that they enjoyed exploring as much as we did, especially when we stopped to admire a view or try to figure out from the geodetic map exactly where we were. Dropping their heads, they casually grazed on wild grasses, at home in the wilderness.

Caves overhang some of these overgrown back trails. Wherever the land levels off, beavers have dammed up a stream to create a pond. Deer, fox, raccoons, and bear abound. The most dramatic sighting we ever made was flushing two fishercats on our way to Bear Pond. We marvelled at moose droppings, each scat the size of a walnut. We heard ruffed grouse drumming, saw ospreys, hawks, and at least a dozen species of songbirds in those far reaches. Sometimes a curious scarlet tanager would accompany us for a mile, flitting from tree to tree as if to point the way. One June day, a bear cub sat in the middle of the path ahead of us. We waited respectfully for it to amble into the woods.

October 21

This is a tense day. I don't know what to expect. Danny comes to drive me to the hospital. Once again I am subjected in my halo to the savageries of the rutted dirt roads.

It is always comforting to travel with Danny. Even if he isn't relaxed he puts up a good front and we manage lighthearted chat during the hour-long trip. He too is a freelance writer, but in the electronic and acoustical fields. A regular contributing editor for several audio-video magazines, he has deadlines to meet. Often he'll call me in a mock-distraught tone to ask if I can hunt up the source of a quote he wants to use. If neither of us can find it, he falls back on "As one nineteenth-century pundit said . . ." Frequently we exchange confidences about writer's block, disagree about a book we have both read, or commiserate about editors who always want a project completed the day after they invented it.

Danny calls me Ma, as opposed to Mom. I think he took this up in his early teens as a gibe directed at the sanctity of motherhood. He was, after all, a child of the sixties. Gradually it evolved into an affectionate term. I've come to depend on him mightily these last six or seven years as I made the transition from typewriter to word processor and from that capability to E-mail. Because his office is in his house, I can almost always consult him when I hit a snag. He tries to be patient with my lack of comprehension; even *Macs for Dummies* is often beyond my intelligence quotient.

Happiest picking away at ideas and concepts on his own, in another era Danny might have been a Talmudic scholar. His work hours may stretch well past midnight, absorb a Sunday, or go by the board for two or three days in a row. Once a week he plays electric guitar in a group; although some are paying gigs, he considers them recreation. In adolescence he studied clarinet, saxophone and bassoon and achieved reasonable proficiency on all. While a student at Bennington College, he played bassoon with the Vermont Symphony, driving to the forty-dollar-a-night rehearsals at opposite ends of the state in his VW Bug. He can fake it, as he likes to say, on the double bass and piano, and once taxed me with the question, "Why didn't you make me take piano lessons?"

"Piano lessons? I couldn't even get you to pick up your underwear," I remember saying.

A music major, he started composing while at Bennington. When Anne Sexton formed her poetry/rock group, "Anne Sexton and Her Kind," Danny provided original music for the background to her poem "The Little Peasant." Still writing music at intervals, he said to me once that what he'd really like to be doing is composing string quartets instead of making a living.

"A couple of centuries ago," he said, "I could have had a patron."

Now he has fruit trees, a few raised vegetable beds

aesthetically placed to enhance the greensward he cultivates, and this coming summer he plans to add an asparagus trench I've promised to supply with three-year-old roots. Baltimore orioles grace his trees. He's quite likely to call me at an odd hour to report on a kingfisher, a saw-whet owl, a scarlet tanager. Wild turkeys are a commonplace now on both our properties, but sighting a fox is rare enough to comment on. Danny is absolutely sure that what woke him two nights in a row last May whiffling around under the bird feeder was a black bear. I am willing to cede him that.

Today I have packed a book bag with pillow, pain pills, and two magazines; this was a good idea because we are put on hold in the waiting room for an hour and a half after we arrive. There is no appropriate chair for a halo-wearer. My discomfort level escalates minute by minute.

First there is a routine standing X ray. Then, the CT scan. My head in a large white doughnut affair, I lie still while the machine takes dozens of cross-sectional pictures of my neck. Then another lengthy wait, as there is "some problem" with the fluoroscope. It requires conscripting every reserve not to panic while I wait to find out whether I am healing or heading for surgery.

Danny is permitted to stay for the fluoroscopy.

They give him a lead apron to put on and he stands on the sidelines, a reassuring presence. The orthopedic surgeon unscrews the bars that run from the halo to the vest, thus liberating my head for the first time in three months. I am then instructed to lean my head back as far as possible, which turns out not to be very far at all. Danny says: "That's about as far back as she was ever able to reach." That seems to satisfy the doctor. Next I am asked to flex the other way. My neck, unused to any movement at all, seems to jitter and wobble the few inches I am able to move it. But before I even try to lower my head, I ask the surgeon, "Can you guarantee my head won't fall off in this maneuver?" Either in humor or as protection against a lawsuit, he responds: "No, I can't guarantee it. But I don't think it will."

Pictures are taken but they are deemed insufficient evidence and the whole procedure has to be repeated. This time I dare to try harder and am able to bend my chin a bit lower. The surgeon overlays the extension and flexion prints and studies them. The bones have not moved. He says that the neck appears stable but he can't figure out why, as there is no physical evidence of fusion. He has never seen this before. He is mystified.

He replaces the bars on the left side of my halo to provide stability, and sends me back for a second CT scan. Danny is not certain that I can lie down on the gurney with only one side of the halo attached, and the technician shares his concern. There is a hasty telephone conference. Then we proceed with the halo still unattached on one side.

Back to the surgeon's office, another lengthy walk from one wing to the next. Danny and I wait for him to study all the films on his light box. Something strange begins to happen to my vision. Lightning jags appear all around the periphery and I recognize I am experiencing the aura that precedes a migraine. This has occurred possibly four times in my life, always triggered by bright sunlight, particularly on snow. But luckily I have never gotten the headache that usually follows an aura.

The surgeon comes back in and announces he is removing the halo. While he is undoing one of the back pins I tell him about the aura, and then, as he moves to the remaining front pin, the whole apparatus releases as if it had been clamped to my skull on springs. The aura vanishes just as suddenly as it appeared. He has no explanation for this phenomenon. In fact, he seems totally uninterested in it. The forehead pin sites are bloody. The surgeon dabs at them with sterile gauze and provides further gauze packs just in case. Then he fits me with a tall rigid foam neck collar, admonishing me that it must never be removed, except for my daily shower, and then only under supervision. He will see me, he says, in a week's time.

I am dumbfounded by my good fortune. Even though surgery has merely been postponed, not positively cancelled, I am out of the halo. I hardly dare move my head the few inches of freedom the collar allows.

"It's like a kid learning to ride a bicycle," he says. "Joyous and scared at the same time."

This is the first empathetic remark he has made. I am touched by it.

It's already two o'clock. We have fifteen minutes before my appointment for an ultrasound of my uterus. It was only when I asked for and received a copy of my medical records, while in the rehab hospital, that I discovered that my family had been worrying about yet another problem. The MRI done shortly after my accident had shown a large mass outside the uterus. My gynecologist was consulted but there was a conspiracy not to tell me about this. It was felt I had enough on my plate.

Today the ultrasound shows no mass, but it does reveal a not very significant fibroid in the upper reaches of the uterus. It is hypothesized that the mass was merely coagulated blood from my rather extensive internal bleeding, and that after thirteen weeks it has been reabsorbed. The radiologist who comes in to give me this news is a rather starchy gentleman with upright bearing and a slight paunch. He wants to know about my accident, how it happened and where. And rather reluctantly, I give him a brief account. I tell him about my friend Kathy, an emergency room nurse in this facility, who saved my life.

"Most people's accidents are quite boring, you know," he says, "but yours is really very interesting. Very interesting! You shouldn't have lived through it and yet here you are."

I murmur some appropriate response.

"As far as I'm concerned," he says, "the only fit place for horses is in an Alpo can."

I am still lying on the examining table and am perfectly positioned to kick this man in the groin. The intravaginal probe still in place restrains me from yielding to the impulse. Meanwhile, Danny has gone to the phone to deliver the good news of postponed surgery and halo removal to Victor, who doesn't answer. He leaves a message on the machine.

It is a little past 4 P.M. when we return home. Judith has just preceded us, having rented a car at the airport after her flight from Geneva. From the expression on her face I can tell that the phone message never got through. We have a giddy reunion, much as if I had just been released from the penitentiary.

That night, lying restlessly awake in this new, stiff restraint, I mull over the surgeon's remark: "I am mystified."

"Je suis mystifié," is what the Swiss obstetrician said when Judith began hemorrhaging three days postpartum. I had flown to Geneva to be her birth partner. Everything seemed to be in order until that third afternoon. Her blood pressure dropped dramatically. As she lay on the gurney preparing for surgery, she made me promise to raise her baby if she didn't survive. Tonight, seventeen years later, I give in to a torrent of tears. That baby is now a junior in high school and Judith has taken a second leave from her UN post to be with me for the spinal fusion surgery that was "pencilled in" and has now been deferred, if not quite cancelled.

Family glue, Victor likes to call it. Judith's son Yann came to stay with us on the farm every summer from the time he was six years old until, at fourteen, he opted for tennis camp. Every June we signed for him at the airport, like a FedEx package, as he came through customs, arriving from Thailand or Yugoslavia or

Germany, wearing the UM (Unaccompanied Minor) tag around his neck.

October 22

     Tonight, in my Philadelphia Tracheotomy Collar—this is its official name, we learn from the enclosed instruction sheet—I prepare to take the first standing-up shower I've had since July 21. Freed of the halo and vest, I feel resplendently naked; with hot water streaming down my back I moan in ecstasy. Judith is monitoring me from her perch on the laundry hamper.

"Do you think this thing [meaning the accident] has improved me morally?" I call out to her.

"What?"

"Morally," I shout over the running water. "You know. Has it made me more patient, kinder, more compassionate?"

"Probably not."

Once I've dried off, she helps me replace the wet collar with the dry one. It is relatively easy to position, we need only center the hole for a tracheotomy over my Adam's apple.

"Now I could go into anaphylactic shock, I suppose," I say. "In case I get stung by a swarm of hornets. They wouldn't even have to take the collar off to save my life."

Judith, ever practical, points out that since we've already had a hard frost, the arrival of hornets is highly unlikely.

October 28

Judith and I gruel back to the critical care hospital for another session of X-ray and flexion/extension tests under fluoroscopy. I am too nervous to eat breakfast. For the last three nights I have been removing the hard collar and substituting a soft foam one so that I can get some sleep, but I am riddled with guilt. What if I have dislocated a mending bone by breaking the rules? On the other hand, I justify this breach of conduct on the grounds that I was frying my brain with sleeping pills as I fought to lose consciousness inside the hideous high collar. I make Judith promise not to bring the subject up until we find out the results of the test.

When we check in at the X-ray department, the ladies behind the desk are wreathed in smiles. They had last seen me in the halo, and one of them had made the unfortunate remark, "Boy, I don't envy you." We have the same cheerful technician as last week, who takes a routine cervical vertical X ray. But when he turns on the fluoroscopy machine its alarm system has been activated and emits a high-pitched screech. He can't figure out how to turn it off and sends us back to the waiting room. When he comes to get us again, he tells us that the problem has been fixed. He put in a call to the manufacturer. The minute an expert came on the line to discuss the problem, the screech vanished. Judith says, "It's just like when you finally make an appointment with the pediatrician. Your kid's fever magically disappears."

The orthopedic surgeon enters. He has already looked at the initial X ray and tells us that it looks just like last week's. It strikes me that this is a strangely neutral way of giving me good news. It is clear he is in the business of not getting people's hopes up and then having to dash them. I take my seat in the chair that is positioned between the two eyes of the fluoroscopy machine. The hard collar is removed and I am urged to tip my head back as far as possible while they watch on the television screens and snap a picture. Then I put my chin as close to my chest as I can and the procedure is repeated. When these two films are developed, he can once again see that the bones are immobile. The fracture line is still clearly visible, but he infers that soft-tissue healing is taking place and possibly the two vertebrae, like two sets of knuckles, have grown together in an unorthodox but useful way.

Greatly relieved, I confess to my sin. I tell him that I slept four nights in the hard collar and had to triple my sleeping medication in order merely to doze off from time to time. The fifth night I replaced the hard brace with a foam neck collar, wedged myself between pillows so I could not turn on my side, and slept in one position on my back. At first, halfway through my confession, he interrupts to say that I must not remove the collar under any circumstance. Then as I describe the soft coffin I prepare to be lowered into, with Victor's hand cradling my head, he relents.

"Okay," he says, "you've passed the garage test."

"The garage test?"

"It's when you've left your car in the garage for a month and you go in and turn the ignition key and it starts right up."

Before we leave, he shepherds us to the secretary's office to arrange another appointment two weeks hence for a third evaluation by lateral cervical X ray, to be followed by fluoroscopy. Two weeks instead of one, the interval he had first suggested—he must have quite a lot of confidence in the healing, I think. Today, his secretary is more than simply cordial; she is effusive. She is going to make sure they are prompt on that date. Didn't she say to Sally last time that it was a shame to keep that poor woman waiting an hour and a half in a halo?

I am no longer faceless, an aggrieved voice on the phone. I suspect that in the future when I dial I will get through.

Now I am finally able to fall asleep without chemical assistance. But the dread that haunted me all those weeks in the rehab hospital, that I would wake in the morning having lost all neurological function, is still present; it's my first waking thought.

In 1980 I lost my beloved brother, the sibling closest to me in age, to ALS, amyotrophic lateral sclerosis, known as Lou Gehrig's disease. We were three years apart in age. Summers, we two were shunted off together to Atlantic City to stay with our grandmother and her companion. A snapshot from that era shows us dressed in white, hair windblown, standing on the boardwalk, frowning identical frowns into the sun. My brother has his left hand in the pocket of his shorts; I have two fingers of the same hand in the strictly-for-decoration pocket of my dress.

Already an engineer, he built elaborate sand castles with spiral pathways down which a tennis ball could run. A willing slave, I fetched endless pails of water to bring the sand to building consistency. Every night the tide came in and carried our castle away. Every morning we would reconstruct it with ever more fanciful additions. Except for my brother, I might have been terribly homesick in exile. In his presence I felt protected and content.

In a poem, I said of our relationship that we "had comforted each other/in the cold zoo of childhood." It took him three years to die. At first he was very brave; as his right side gradually weakened, he fruitlessly worked various gripping devices to preserve his right hand, and he had his shoes modified with Velcro straps so that he could fasten them with his left. And to me privately he vowed that as soon as the disease showed any sign of moving to his other side, he would take his own life.

I suppose every terminally ill person, given sufficient notice, makes a similar vow. I know that I would. I even went so far, presurgery, as to E-mail a very close doctor friend in a distant city and ask him to agree to put me down if I awakened post-surgery a quadriplegic. I am not depressed and I am not insane, I wrote to him, I have made my wishes very clear to all the family, but I think they are too emotionally involved to take action. So don't lecture me; just E-mail me one word, yes or no. And to his everlasting credit he fired back the one word: yes.

In my brother's case, he was unable to act in time. Perhaps the life force was so strong that he decided against it, or he had a failure of nerve, or the ministrations of his only son, who left graduate school and came home to care for his father, convinced him to hang on. I flew out to California every month. Much of our relationship is detailed in my poems about him—my dreams about his recovery, his trips to the therapy pool, my pushing him in the wheelchair to see the new trees leafing out his final spring. By then he could no longer talk. For a little while he could write questions on a child's slate, but soon he lacked the motor skill even for this. Toward the end, each time I saw him he would feebly draw his index finger across his throat in what I took to be a mute appeal to me to help him end his ordeal. I regret that I was a coward. Finally, he caught pneumonia and the doctors, who had been, I thought, astonishingly indifferent to his suffering, decided not to treat the disease. Pneumonia, the old man's friend, they said. And so he was left to drown in his own fluids. He was sixty.

I carry my brother's story around with me like a very heavy knapsack. First he lost the use of his legs, then his arms, then his ability to speak, and finally even his fingers turned to stone. I am trying to make provisions for my own exit just as he did. But probably just as he could not rely on me, I will not be able to rely even on my faithful friend of the one-word E-mail.

October 29

Today, with the surgeon's imprimatur I am permitted to go into the therapy pool for my PT session. The temperature of the water is ninety-five degrees; going down the stairs into the four-foot depth is comforting, especially to my hands and feet, where my circulation has been compromised ever since the accident. Wendy paces the deck like Ahab, ordering me to walk forward, backward, sideways with squats between steps, and so on. The arm coordination is a little tricky and I have to stop and start in order to get it right. In the far corner where the water is over my head, I wear a flotation belt and tread water as if I were riding a bicycle. Forty-five minutes in the pool is an exhausting workout, yet I have done nothing but walk and move my legs, certainly nothing that would threaten the stability of my neck.

Oddly, I don't feel constrained in this tiny, warm pool. It doesn't compare with the Olympic-size pools I have worked out in, except in intensity, or the distance swims I undertook in my youth. During my college years, I worked summers on the waterfront of a camp in the Berkshires. Every morning I slipped naked into the lake and swam a mile before breakfast, a delicious exertion I wrote about in a poem called "Morning Swim." It ends: "My bones drank water. Water fell/through all my doors. I was the well/that met the lake that met my sea/in which I sang 'Abide with Me.'" That dawn overhand across the lake was just about as tiring as today's session for this cripple.

Wendy says that she wishes "these orthopedic doctors" would spend just ten minutes in a rehab facility to see what the therapists are doing. This applies particularly to the pool, which provides a safe medium for recovering joints. "Some of them," she says, "think we're *swimming* in here." After I've dried off she helps me exchange my wet collar for my dry one.

In today's mail a letter from my writer/horse friend Ann Jones, who is out in Arizona working away on a new book. She will soon leave for a travel-writing assignment in the Middle East—her bread and butter between books—and about my accident she says, "I'm not surprised to learn that you go on writing when confined to the rack [the halo]. I'm sure you're one of those people who would be brilliantly courageous under torture, spitting in the eye of your interrogator, and all that."

At least she is not praying for me, as are so many others, to wit: "I do not believe God is, or ever was, angry at you. He loves you so much that He is beside himself with joy [at the halo removal]. Of course this accident was in His scheme of things, but it is my experience that whenever a person leads a good and holy life as you have, God wishes to bring this person even closer to Him in a kind of 'endurance of love' and while it might seem and even be terrible from our point of view, it is really a kind of Glory of Love in which we find ourselves. I had to learn the hard way that God wanted me to surrender to Him and relax in His arms. I believe He wants this of you."

Oh, to have a faith as staunch as this devout fan. Lucky, lucky true believers. I had elicited this letter by supposing sardonically that I should thank God for relenting in time to spare me surgery.

Not only am I prayed for daily at Catholic mass by

my admirer, but I am called to the Almighty's attention by some Episcopalians in Tennessee, Quakers in Florida, a Buddhist/Baptist in California, and a dear old Mormon friend in Salt Lake City. It isn't that I haven't thought about God. After all, I had all those years of Sunday school in a Reform Jewish temple in Philadelphia. I went to synagogue with my parents and siblings and fasted on Yom Kippur and picked black walnut nutmeats out of their hard shells to help make the German-style charoses for the Seder meal. But my religion was largely a kitchen religion.

At about sixteen I became a deist, crediting God with creating and then abandoning the universe. By the end of my freshman year at Radcliffe, a college then considered heretical by many, I had shed even my deism for agnosticism. My agnosticism eroded eventually to the skeletal remains of atheism and there I still stand. I'm not sure whether I should envy or pity the faith of others. Yes, it would be nice to have, but it seems a luxury of pietism that I cannot afford. I said to Judith once that although I had a near-death experience, there was neither an angel nor a Lucifer lurking in the corridor. In fact, there was no corridor, no guiding light. When he heard this, Danny remarked, "Maybe you just weren't near enough."

October 30

I was itching yesterday when I got out of the pool; today I am itching even more. By 5 P.M. I wish I could tear the skin off my neck and back. The collar is intolerable and I take it off, only to reveal an angry rash that runs from my hairline to my waist and has spread to my chest. Of course it's a Friday. My internist's office is closed. Luckily, the internist on call for the weekend is an activist. She orders 30 milligrams of prednisone, to be decreased by 5 milligrams each day, as well as a powerful though sleep-inducing antihistamine. Victor, who is a retired chemical engineer, wonders whether I have developed an allergy to the flowing agent used to make the foam of the collar. "Let's get hold of the surgeon and see if there's some other collar, one made out of something else."

Judith suggests to the internist on call that as a colleague she might have better luck reaching him than the patient or members of the patient's family might.

"I'll give it a try," she says cheerfully. But in ten minutes she calls back to say that he is out of town for the weekend.

"They're always out of town for the weekend," I mutter.

November 2

Monday. Victor spends the morning on the phone with the company that manufactures the Philadelphia Collar, discussing the possible etiology of my rash. At around noon, the surgeon calls. I am still itching but the severity has diminished and the rash is fading. I ask him if he has ever seen this kind of reaction before; he says he has seen a sweat rash under the collar but nothing so generalized. He suggests that I dispense with the hard collar and just use the soft foam one, except for riding in the car, walking, and working out in PT or with weights. I am greatly relieved.

"Anything else?" he asks.

At this point I am lying on the bed, holding the phone to my ear. "Let me ask my hovering family," I say.

"Ah, a conference call. You've got a speaker phone there?"

So he does have a sense of humor.

I pass the phone to Judith, who receives the same instructions. When she hangs up she turns to me. "I think we're training this guy."

Judith returns to Geneva, laptop and all. For the last ten days she has called up her E-mail first thing in the morning and worked her way through about fifty messages a day. Some of these were simply Reuters news dispatches, but a great many others required diligent attention. She wrote an article, she wrote a speech, she exchanged pleasantries with colleagues and ran her office long distance. Often at night I would lie in bed across the hall from my study and listen to the clack clack of the laptop keyboard as she maintained contact with a life beyond the farm and its inhabitants. I have always admired her ability to keep a foot in two worlds, to tack up and ride her father's old broodmare in the afternoon and tend to the next day's UN business in the evening. The keys sounded like small seashells tumbling together as a wave brought them to shore, a gently erratic music.

I am trying to learn how to say goodbye gracefully, without burdening her with my dependence. She will try to come back in February, she says. But to me, three intervening months stretch like an empty desert.

November 6

The news is full of the devastation wrought in Central America by Hurricane Mitch, the storm of the century. The death toll is already enormous—ten thousand in Honduras alone—but the numbers go up by the minute. Of all the commentary on the scene, the interviews with weathermen specializing in hurricanes, with harried aid workers lamenting the shortage of helicopters, I see only one commentator face the camera and tell the bald truth. Last year and the year before, he said, Central America experienced a terrible drought. Not only did it destroy crops, it killed all the vegetation. When the hurricane struck and the rains came, the bare hills gave way and mud slides swept down into the valleys where the little villages were, obliterating them. *Classic greenhouse effect,* he said, enunciating the words very carefully. And then they cut him off. To acknowledge an act of God is one thing, but to acknowledge human responsibility is another.

November 8

VIPs from around the world converge on Central America. "Disaster tourism," Judith calls it. As aid workers must take time off from saving lives to shepherd foreign ministers and first ladies through the rubble, such tourism hinders the relief effort. The television news is a succession of interviews with villagers who have lost everything: homes, livestock, children. I remember my own bout with the "compassion junkies" and can imagine, at least to some extent, how these bereft people must feel.

November 10

The closer I get to November 12, the more my anxiety builds. This will be my third evaluation by X ray and fluoroscopy and I think I am more terrified than ever. *What if*, my brain plays over and over. What if the bones have shifted after all and I must undergo surgery to fuse C1 and C2? Why didn't we get this over with on October 26 as planned? If we had, I would now be three weeks down the road to recovery. I've read about this surgery in Christopher Reeve's book, *I'm Still Me*; at least I tried to read his detailed description but turned away in fear. It was too graphic.

When my surgeon was first mulling over the mystery of my seemingly stable neck, he said, "It would be a shame to open you up and find the bones had fused on their own."

He didn't expatiate on this thought; he didn't have to. Knowing that this operation begins with a deep incision in the hip to access necessary live bone for the repair, I am horrified by the possible scenario. Having come this far, I ought to be thinking positively. I ought to believe in my body's ability to heal itself. Even if C1-C2 have grown together in a funny offset arthritic way, I have outfoxed the fates who so cruelly severed Reeve's spinal cord but were content merely to bruise mine.

November 12

This is a rerun of October 28. The results of the X rays are identical.

Today, after overlaying the flexion and extension plates, the surgeon is positively jocular. "I don't know who's looking after you," he says half humorously, half incredulously. "It looks like somebody is on your side."

"Can you see where they're fused?"

"No. We may never see where. But there's absolutely no movement, not a millimeter in any direction."

Now I am to discard the high collar except when travelling over dirt roads and abandon the soft one indoors much of the time. I am to begin gentle range of motion with my neck: up, down, and side to side. In OT/PT the therapists will gradually help me hold my head straight (I am still tilted to the left from all those weeks in the halo). As for the decreased sensation and function in my right hand and fingers, maybe I will get them back, maybe not. He will repeat the X rays in one month. Am I out of the woods? He will not say definitively.

That afternoon, Wendy, my PT, says that dealing with spinal cord injuries is like dealing with a death. The patient must go through the same stages of anger, denial, and so on, to acceptance of his or her limitations.

Nevertheless, she is quite adamant: "You will get it back, you will get it all back." She removes my collar, squats down in front of me and tells me to lift my chin. I do so, possibly an inch. Then, under instruction, I lower my chin, possibly two inches. But the side to side motion evades me.

"What's stopping you?" she asks.

"Terror," I reply. She assures me that my muscles will keep me from turning too far. Bone will not grind upon bone. It is perfectly safe to turn my head.

That evening I turn my head a little more. When I wake toward dawn, I take the collar off. I still cannot turn on my side without considerable pain on the opposite side of my neck, but I remind myself how relatively comfortable this position is compared to the steady torture of the halo.

November 16

～～～ Over the last couple of weeks I've begun to write poems again, after a long hiatus. I'd like to do a whole series in this setting; maybe others will come. Couldn't there be an amputees poem? I've met so many cheerful, upbeat men, mostly advanced diabetics, but some of them trauma patients, skillfully maneuvering their wheelchairs in between therapy sessions or getting fitted for and learning how to walk on prostheses. Those who have been without legs for a long time have immensely muscular upper torsos and massive arms. They adapt to their artificial limbs by inching along between the parallel bars. Why not a poem about the brain damaged, having to relearn the act of standing and then walking? Why do I leave myself out of these prospective poems? Why do I think the halo is too specialized—too painfully immediate—for a poem?

In the Rehab Hospital

Their wheelchairs are Conestoga wagons drawn
into the arc of a circle at 2 P.M.

Elsie, Gladys, Hazel, Fanny, Dora
whose names were coinage after the First World War

remember their parents tuned to the Fireside Chats,
remember in school being taught to hate the Japs.

They sit attentive as seals awaiting their fish
as the therapist sings out her cheerful directives:

Square the shoulders, lean back, straighten the knee
and lift. Tighten and lift. Up, up, and away!

They will retrain the side all but lost in a stroke,
the spinal cord mashed but not severed in traffic,

they will learn to adjust to their newly replaced
hips, they will walk on feet of shapely plastic.

This darling child in charge of their destiny
will lead them forward across the prairie.

IV

November 20

It's a day shy of four months since my accident. Today I have an appointment with the rheumatologist who has been monitoring my arthritis for the last several years. He takes the time to test all my reflexes—"a little brisk," he reports, in keeping with neuron damage—diagnoses the lump on my right shoulder as a separation that requires no treatment at the moment, examines the indentation across my upper arm and pronounces it a deep muscle tear. He is less equivocal and more forthcoming about the final outcome than my surgeon, but the difference is probably one of temperament, not of substance. He warns me that the first two months post-halo is the critical period, but that even after that I am not cleared for takeoff. Six months, he says, would be a reasonable time frame. He also orders some blood work to rule out anemia but doesn't think my complaint of fatigue is unreasonable. "You're a fighter," he says. "Look how far you've come."

November 22

"Spinal cord injuries are like snowflakes. No two are the same," my PT is fond of saying. Part of what is frightening is this very uniqueness. I cannot extrapolate from anyone else's experience. I have to go it alone. Like dying, this is a journey on which no one can accompany me. No matter how sympathetic, no matter how helpful or patient or slow to anger the members of my family are, it's my snowflake.

November 23

Last night Victor and I watched the videotape of Dr. Jack Kevorkian euthanizing an ALS sufferer. This morning the controversy is swirling through all of the newscasts. Special commentaries are provided by spokesmen for the Church, ethics professors, and relatives of desperately ill patients who begged for release. Those who are outraged find the filming of the death morally repugnant, aesthetically offensive. But I am offended by their squeamishness. What about live scenes of carnage in civil war? The marketplace massacre in Sarajevo, Rwandans hacked to death? The television screen is crowded with morally repugnant images every day.

Victor and I are on opposite sides of this issue. He is opposed to the overt act, which is murder, but not wholly against doctor-assisted suicide, provided it is done discreetly (which is, after all, the way it is usually done). I think this position is casuistic; I think the terminally ill have a right to die by their own hand or the hand of a selected other. To me, it is morally repugnant to draw a line between which hand actually pushes the plunger. As the poet and political commentator Katha Pollitt put it in another context, we must "resist the heaving tide of sanctimonious flotsam."

December 7

Hunting season ended yesterday; for the first time since last summer, we are free to walk in our woods. Nature is abetting my slow recovery. An unusually warm late fall has made it possible for me to get out almost every day. Usually, Victor and I walk up past the pond to our driving dressage ring with its one-eighth-of-a-mile track, and trudge around it. By adding a boring lap each day I've worked up to a mile on these legs that feel foreign, heavy, wrapped in canvas cloth. The dogs go with us; then, obviously disappointed by our tame journey, wander off to explore the surrounding woods.

This promises to be an unseasonable Indian summer day, the last of its kind. We agree to tackle the back trail that winds through the woods from the bottom of our farthest field to an adjoining farm's pastures and hidden pond, then out to the bottom road and back uphill to our house. It's a three-mile loop with only a few hills, a scenic route we once used as a mild warm-up on horseback. How many sunshine patriots—city visitors—I took on this gentle excursion! Boomer with an innocent passenger on her back was content to amble along behind my horse until we stopped in the neighboring farm's field above the pond to let the horses graze. Often we'd flush a family of deer or put up some ducks that lived on the pond's little island. Once we got out to the road I'd snap a lead shank on Boomer's bridle so that she couldn't carry the benevolent greenhorn off at a gallop, and we would continue our decorous pace homeward.

Today I think my own legs can manage the first stretch, as far as the fields and pond. Possibly, after a rest period, I'll be able to hike on out to the now-deserted farmhouse. It's sunny and warm and I can simply sit down on a convenient outcropping and rest as necessary. Victor says he will go fetch the car for the drivable portion of the return. To my amazement and delight, I am able to make the entire trip on my own, stopping only twice: once by the pond with its little island, and farther on to sit in the sun with Victor on the stone wall by the farmhouse.

"I feel like I just finished the Boston Marathon," I say.

"Get ready for tomorrow," he teases. "We're going to jog up Mount Kearsarge."

It's a small event that magnifies into a big victory for me. Never mind how arduous it was. If I could do this walk, I think, once I get up to speed I will be able to wander all over our back trails.

We are both a little sad, looking back over the intervening years. When we first came to New Hampshire in 1963, this once-handsome home was owned by a Swiss couple who cherished every inch of it. The lawns were mowed, the huge barn was immaculate, the open fields were "brushed out" every year or so to keep the weed trees from taking over. Whenever we rode through from our farm we received a warm welcome.

What were once rolling fields and pine forests have now been clear-cut and trashed. The farmhouse, which dates back to the late 1700s, has fallen into disrepair. The cavernous barn, where we once stored our surplus hay, is no longer weatherproof. The last owners filed for personal bankruptcy and decamped in a hurry, leaving bales of spoiled hay and piles of cow manure and sawdust bedding along the road. "I record only the sunny hours," says the inscription on the sundial.

December 10

Back to the orthopedic surgeon once again, Danny at the wheel. By now, I am well known to the hospital receptionists in X-ray.

The last time we were here, a Frenchwoman was waiting in some bewilderment at the desk for an interpreter. "I don't know what's keeping her," the receptionist said with some exasperation.

I offered my modest gift: "Je peux parler français mais lentement et mal," and was able to relay the technician's simple instructions.

Today, I go to the front of the line. The same routine is followed. Once the X rays are developed, we trudge over to the surgeon's office where he spreads them out on his light box and prepares to discuss the three views, the cervical vertical, extension, and flexion.

Although the fracture line is still clearly visible, nothing has changed. "It may look like that forever," he says. "But you're out of the woods."

I feel light-headed with relief; truly, I am healed.

Although there is still no clear evidence of where

the bones have fused, he has some ideas about the location. The two surfaces of the vertebrae have probably sandpapered themselves together, either in front or along one side. In surgery they follow much the same procedure, abrading the surfaces they are going to connect. Bleeding bone, as it is called, stimulated in this way, encourages the two pieces to grow together. It also appears likely that a portion of C2, the thumb-like structure that sticks up through C1 and was broken at midpoint, may have attached itself to the side of the top vertebra. Next spring he would like to repeat the X rays and redo the CT scan, more in the interest of science than to be sure I have mended.

"You're a walking miracle," he tells me. "Consider this a rebirth."

What he goes on to say I am not really ready to hear. "Ninety-five percent of people with your fracture never make it to the emergency room. Ninety-five percent of the ones who do, end up as quadriplegics."

That's how close I came to the abyss. I haven't let myself think about it before this pronouncement, though certainly I have known "how fine a line exists/between buoyance and stone" and for a long time after the accident I wished fiercely that I had crossed over. Getting better was such an ordeal; by contrast, death looked so easy. Once they got used to the idea of my death, I thought, it would have spared my family all the arrangements, elaborations and undertakings that surrounded my convalescence.

Now I am supposed to be grateful for getting my life back, even with its impairments. I am told over and over by various friends and acquaintances that God spared me. That he had something else in mind for me. I am torn between amusement and foreboding. What he has in mind might not be some Joan of Arc role. Perhaps I am only saved alive, the fundamentalists would say, to be roasted over the coals of hell.

Why aren't I suffused with gratitude and well-being? What's the matter with me that I don't wake up each morning glad to be here, why am I still a little doubtful that this is the better bargain? With Rilke I can "await the birth-hour of a new clarity," but it is hard for me to "keep holy all that befalls." What befell me is still so daunting that I can't own up to it. I want to replay it, do it over, not let it happen. If denial precedes acceptance, I fear I am still in denial, tinged with anger and grief for my lost capacities.

Chronic pain is part of the reason. It is hard to be cheerful when your neck and back cause continual pain. Chances are that some degree of discomfort is permanent. Chances, too, that my numb right hand and reduced arm strength are here to stay. I still cannot do buttons or hooks and eyes; earrings are out of the question. I need two hands to lift a carton of milk out of the refrigerator. Preparing even a simple meal requires not only twice as much time as it once did but also prodigious patience. Chopping, stirring, transferring ingredients have become monumental tasks.

Although I am able to provide minimal horse care, putting horses in their stalls and distributing their grain in the morning, it is clear that I am not going to be able to tend our foursome on my own. The heavier-duty barn chores I once relished—mucking out, hauling water buckets, spreading sawdust bedding—are still beyond my capacity.

Sliding stall latches is something I can manage, but fastening and unfastening snap hooks is something else. And each of our stall doors is outfitted with a backup double-ended snap hook, a necessity for living with smart Arabians with prehensile noses. Otherwise, they lean over their stall doors, let each other out, and create mayhem. They double up in each other's stalls, bat the open doors back and forth, bending or even breaking hinges. Even the light switch sports a protective cover; Victor installed this after we awakened several mornings to a barn ablaze with wattage and accused each other of having forgotten to turn the lights out.

My brain cells seem to be as stubbornly fertile as they were in what the medical profession calls my "premorbid state." For this I am properly grateful. Being able to transfer thought to words is what saved me during that long spell in the hospital. Even when I was at my most vulnerable, unable to use my hands or fingers, I could speak my state of mind to Judith, at the ready with her laptop.

As for my writing life, I am able to use the typewriter fairly easily, the computer keyboard with some difficulty. I came unwillingly to the computer, chivvied into learning how to use its word-processing ability by Danny. For a long time I printed out two copies of every po-biz letter I wrote, filing the second copy in my desk under "Speaking Upcoming," "Recommendations and Blurbs," or "Reprint Permissions." Then Danny installed a letterhead and showed me how to use it. Grudgingly and full of doubt, I began to let the letters folder take over the tedium of hand-filing copies. I am still only semi-literate but now look with pity on some of my old Luddite friends who haven't yet made the leap. My neighbor Donald Hall, on the other side of Mount Kearsarge, is still resisting the new age. "But I have a dedicated fax!" he tells me. "Deeply dedicated!" We both love the sound of it.

"You're still using a typewriter?" people ask incredulously. I write poems on my old IBM Selectric, running each revision through a new draft on a new page. Every time I retype a poem it magically shrinks or grows or rearranges itself in the actual physical process, not always for the best. But a poem is not a watercolor; it doesn't turn muddy and have to be abandoned after twenty minutes. The poet can always go back to an earlier version if she writes beyond the ending, as sometimes happens. All those typed drafts spread out on the desk suggest endless possibilities.

I cannot imagine doing this on a computer. But there's no unanimity among poets. Most contemporary poets, at least the younger ones, compose on their PCs or Macs. Others compose only in longhand on yellow legal pads. Some brag they never rewrite. Their poems come in ten minutes (Archie Ammons has a good poem about writing a poem in this time span). Still others claim they've spent seven years on one long poem. I'm a heavy reviser but I try to know when to quit. What matters is the poem, not the poet.

December 21

◢◣ Five months exactly since the catastrophe.
The winter solstice arrives. We have abundant snow
flurries though no serious accumulation. Both wood-
stoves are going. It's dark by 4 P.M. I bundle up and go
out with Victor, now that the mares are gone, to feed
our two stalwarts, Boomer and Deuter. The latter snug-
gles his head under my armpit in the old way, his standard show of affection, asking to have his ears stroked.
We stand around a few minutes in the yellow glow of
lamplight, taking turns feeding carrots. I take off my useless glove and bury my dead right hand in the fur under
Deuter's red mane. His animal warmth comforts me.

December 22

◢◣ We are inundated with holiday greeting cards
from well wishers, many of them featuring horses and
sleighs. Some distant friends with whom we exchange
greetings only once a year still do not know about my
accident. I sigh, dreading the explanatory letters I now
feel obliged to write.

Victor did all the notifying in the first weeks after I
was hospitalized. His messages were unfailingly upbeat:

"Max is now into her fourth week of recovery. . . . The physical rehab has been terrific. The orthopedic consultant was in and she put on quite a performance for him, both intellectually and physically."

In another communiqué: "Her assignments have all been cancelled through 1998 with the hope that 1999 will be a return to productive work beginning with the two-month teaching stint in Florida, January and February. Her attitude is terrific! She is determined to return, to get her strength back, and we are now confident *we* [italics mine] will."

Christmas Day

Low-key; a feast at Danny's, token presents (the new P. D. James mystery in paperback, a clock that produces birdsongs instead of hourly chimes). Real gifts for Noah, whose ninth birthday precedes today by a scant two weeks. To be born in December, as Noah was or in January like Judith's son Yann, I think, has to rub some of the luster from this holiday.

Travel by car is still an act of penance for me. At the mercy of my querulous neck muscles and tendons, I can't sit comfortably anywhere for very long. Danny worries about the impending flight to Florida. So do I,

though I don't admit it. His wife gives me a back pillow
that folds like a triptych.

December 31

Victor uncorks a really good white Bordeaux
and we bid the old year goodbye with no regrets. I am
trying to prepare for the next seven weeks in the trop-
ics. My severely compromised circulation needs some
respite from the cold, but I hate leaving the farm.

January 6

Victor and I fly off to Miami. In line at the gate, I refuse to load in advance with the elderly impaired and families with small children; I consider it demeaning, but snag two airline pillows on the way to my seat. We arrive on time, disgorged into the bedlam of Miami International Airport, and then wait in line for over an hour to pick up our prepaid rental car.

It's almost dark before we arrive at the pied-à-terre, the same one where I stayed last year. A studio apartment at the back end of a house in a small gated community, it opens onto a private terrace surrounded by palms and flowering shrubs. I am grateful to be back; it seems essential to my well-being to be able to open a door and put my feet on the bare, unsnowy ground. High-rise condos on Miami Beach hold no charms; I have no desire to overlook the ocean with its unceasing sameness. Let others be seduced by the rise and fall of waves, the perpetual mustache of foam along the tide line, the ever-present seam of horizon, the constant wind. I need to be enclosed in greenery as if by mountains. I enjoy the chitter of surrounding palm fronds, scrub jays cawing from the trees, the comfort of growth and bloom.

January 8

Until now, I've been cosseted by family and friends who opened doors, fastened my seat belt, even peered left or right whenever I pulled out into an intersection. ("You can't drive any worse than the other drivers in Miami," the orthopedic surgeon remarked ominously when he granted me clearance to get behind the wheel.) Today, in late afternoon, I drive myself to the campus of Florida International University to get my parking permit, pick up any mail that accumulated this week, and meet briefly with the students who've signed up for my advanced poetry workshop in the M.F.A. program. Maneuvering myself in and out of the car, inching my way up the stairs to the creative writing program office (I am still too claustrophobic to dare the elevator without someone at my side) exacts all my strength and resolve. I have to walk through several connecting buildings to sign for the parking decal, then trudge back to the parking lot to affix it to my rear bumper. I can't believe I am doing all this on my own. I am exhausted to the point of pain by the time I get back to my digs.

This is going to be heavy duty. Whatever it takes, I'm determined to make it work. I worry that Victor will be bored by our insularity here, that he will grow restive from what Willa Cather called the "innumerable shades of sweetness and anguish" that characterize our daily lives here.

January 10

Everybody checks in by phone this Sunday: Jane and Scott from San Francisco; Judith from Geneva; Danny, who reports on the third ice storm of the season in New Hampshire. I take advantage of my five-cents-a-minute Sunday service to call several old friends. Last of all I call Nicole, who has just moved into a more accessible house. They've eliminated a closet in order to make one bathroom door wide enough to accommodate the wheelchair. The formal dining room has become her study. Her computer is up but her husband still has to install a phone jack before she can reestablish E-mail contact.

"You'll be the first one I write to," she says.

The biggest news is her new car, which is modified to operate with hand controls. Her wheelchair goes in a carrier on the roof. There's a ramp down to the garage. Now she can go places, along with her little boy.

"I have to put a leash on him," she says. "I hate doing it, but he could just run out into the street while I'm getting the car door open."

"I know, I raised three of them and I had legs! I can't imagine how you're doing all this on your own."

"Well, it works. And now I can get out as long as it's not icy. I even do the grocery shopping myself."

"You mean in one of those little electric carts?"

"No, they don't hold enough. I just push a regular cart ahead of me with one hand and steer my chair with the other."

I picture Nicole with her cart and chair scooting down the aisles of the local Market Basket. Other customers step back as she sweeps past.

"How's the hand?" she asks.

"Maybe a little better. Not much change. It's almost six months."

Her six-month date is in February. She says the day she toppled from the ladder seems much longer ago. A year, at least. Two years.

"Sometimes I think about walking," she says. "I try to remember what it felt like. You wouldn't think I could forget so soon, would you?"

January 12

We walk around this gated community once, sometimes twice a day. Last year I power-walked an hour early every morning, circling the perimeter and adding in a couple of extra loops to fill out the time. This year, thirty minutes exhausts me. Paradoxically, I find walking on asphalt on flat terrain more challenging than negotiating the humps and hills of our backwoods. Here, I am more conscious of a sort of hitch in my gait, an internal unsteadiness that may not be discernible to others but which requires all my concentration to mask. I am very self-conscious. People can see how clumsy I am, how crippled, unable to stand up straight.

January 15

My computer is working and the printer is printing. I am able to work for an hour or so at a time before I crash; lying flat is the best relief for this constant nag of neck and shoulder pain. My fingers are much more agile on the keys now, a big improvement over two months ago. Warm weather makes a significant difference.

Workshop is shaping up. It's still hard to see exactly how it's going to fly, but another week should tell. No problem learning names and faces this year. It helps to have four former students on board. No one has rebelled at the prospect of memorizing a poem a week and explicating same before reciting it to the class. I'm glad I'm not teaching an assortment of precocious undergraduates; they are always hard to win over. This group is composed of adults, people who are out in the world holding down jobs, and sitting up late to prepare their assignments. They have to love what they are doing almost as much as I, longtime poetry evangelist, do.

January 20

Victor flew home this morning. On the theory that there would be no traffic tie-ups in midmorning and midweek, I somewhat trepidatiously drove him to the airport. He has been replaced as my caretaker by Debbie Brown, who arrived this evening and will stay for ten days. I wish I were not so needy; I still can't do buttons, apply paper clips, get the tops off most jars, or fish change out of the zipper compartment of my wallet. Driving the car is not difficult except for getting the key into the ignition and the tongue of the seat belt into place. I am extra wary of left turns and swivel halfway around in my seat to make sure I can see oncoming traffic.

January 21

We celebrate the six-month milestone—"after six months you're in the clear," my rheumatologist had said—with chilled stone crab claws, which Debbie has never tasted. I assure her that since she likes lobster, she'll love these. Lacking crackers and picks, we utilize a hammer and pliers from the toolshed, making up in gusto what we lack in elegance. I'm remembering a friend's celebration of the fifth anniversary of her mastectomy—"after five years, you're in full remission," her surgeon had said—with champagne and caviar. I yearn to feel the same assurance. For a long time I have been dogged by the neurotic fear that I might still lose neurological function. But at this six-month milestone I am determined to give up this lingering obsession.

As a near-sighted small child I was taken twice a year to the ophthalmologist. This venerable German gentleman would insert one lens after another in the heavy metal frame that sat precariously on my nose. One eye at a time, he would ask: "Iss ziss better or iss ziss vurse? Better or vurse?" I would take a long time to decide. Was it better? Was it worse? Or was it just the same? *Same* was not an option.

Every morning I ask myself these questions. Is my neck better or worse? (*Same* is not an option.) My right hand, any change? What about my legs, which still feel wooden and swathed in some awning-like material? When I walk, striving to look normal, is the woolly sensation better or worse?

February 6

True to her promise, Judith flies in from Switzerland for a week. She casts an approving eye around my little apartment, then goes out onto the terrace. After weeks of gray skies in Geneva, she is happy to soak up some sunshine, and I am inordinately happy that the weather is cooperating.

I've been totally on my own for the last seven days and find that I can worm my way around most obstacles to independent living. These include corkscrew, vegetable peeler, the cords of ceiling fans, manila envelopes that have been taped closed, and the metal snaps on skirt or trouser hangers. But now that she's here, Judith takes over. I am happy to have her run my life. She sections the grapefruit, she drives the car, she discovers a bakery with New York–style bagels, a Thai restaurant, a mall with an enormous bookstore and café. Together, we will visit friends, eat out, and actually see a movie— my first, I realize, in almost a year.

February 13

I drive Judith to the airport for her early evening return flight. I've made this run often enough now so that despite Miami's maze of interlocking highways, I am able to thread my way without getting rattled. Miami drivers as a group are profoundly intolerant of snowbirds. They lean on their horns, crowd you at lights, and even pull alongside to make menacing gestures. I've learned how to merge with the traffic, find my lane and stay in it.

It is still excruciatingly hard to see Judith go. For years we've had a little ritual. Hugging her, I say, "Why couldn't you just have moved to the next town and raised goats?" And she replies, "Well, I would have, Mom. But you brought me up all wrong."

In any case, she'll be back in April. There's a good chance that she will spend next year in the States or in Canada. I watch her walk to the airport door, turn and wave; I say to myself, next year in America.

February 28

Victor has come back for my final week of classes. He's repackaged the computer and printer, the carton of books I brought with me, plus an extra carton of books I've acquired over the past two months, and arranged a pickup time with FedEx. The return flight takes place without incident. But two minutes of exposure to New England weather between airport and car and my hands and feet turn to stone.

March 15

I'm getting up early every morning now to bring the horses in. There's still snow underfoot. I crutch my way down the icy road with a ski pole, duck through the paddock fence, and receive a warm greeting from Boomer and Deuter. So far, all I am able to do is invite each into his stall in the order they've long since established. Their morning hay was tucked into each stall last night, so I distribute the grain ration and check all the latches before I pole my way back to the house. The mares are coming home today, which will intensify my labors. I know I can manage, though. Every morning I try lifting the manure fork; any day now, I'm going to start mucking out the motel lobby they've lounged in most of the night.

March 30

Spring still feels like a distant dream; nevertheless, I've started an array of vegetable seeds in my habitual warmed nursery on top of the refrigerator. Once they sprout, they go under fluorescent lights. A new red pepper cultivar looks sturdy, as do the cherry tomatoes. About two hundred onion seeds have germinated. Cabbage, broccoli, cauliflower, and brussels sprouts are all emerging on schedule in their square-inch cells of soil.

After every member of the family has approached me singly and for the most part tactfully, I've agreed to let the two young mares go off on free lease. While I don't want them to stand around all summer as mere lawn ornaments, I'm not ready to cut the cord completely. A lease means I can take them back if the arrangement sours; no one can sell them down the river. Praise will go to the lawyer daughter of my old poet friend Philip Booth. Lu is going to join the equine herd at SUNY Cobleskill. She'll be used in carriage-driving classes and become the director's own competitive trail horse. Boomer and Deuter, Victor says, go with the farm. They're here to stay as long as we.

April 18

Nicole and her little boy are coming today for Sunday brunch. It seems we've been planning this reunion for months. Danny and Libby and Noah are coming, too. I've made a fresh fruit cup, set the table, assembled the bacon, and stayed out of Victor's way as he prepared his culinary masterpiece, genuine sourdough waffle batter.

When she arrives, the dogs and I come out to admire Nicole's newly equipped car. We watch the clever mechanism that slides open the chair carrier atop the roof, then lowers her wheelchair beside the car's open door. Very matter-of-factly, she reaches down to snap the folding seat open and lock the chair wheels, then lifts her legs into position. With one deft heave of both arms she's out of the car and seated in the chair.

I reflect that she does this several times a day, but despite her insouciance I doubt that she ever takes it for granted. Learning how to transfer, she once told me, she'd fallen to the ground several times. It's one thing for me to stand here and admire her agility. Public approval in no way matches the price that she pays daily.

Little Paul, blond and apple-cheeked, is asleep in his car seat in the back. "He'll wake up in a second," she assures me. "He won't want to miss anything." She opens the back door, croons to him till his eyes open, then unsnaps his safety belt. She rolls up the leash he wears around his waist and tucks it into his pocket. He climbs down himself. Easing him, trailing his security blanket, onto her lap, she wheels in front of the car onto the lawn to greet Victor.

It's a bright blue-sky day. For weeks lying side by side in our hospital beds, she and I talked so much about the farm; I can't wait to show Nicole around.

"How about a guided tour by golf cart?" I say. "We bought this used one last spring for trucking stuff back and forth to the garden."

Victor extracts the cart from its winter berth in the barn. We worry it won't start after all this time, but the motor comes to life, first with a series of pings, then a succession of gratifying putt-putts. Once again, Nicole makes a swift transfer. Paul, who has clambered down while she swings herself into the cart, wordlessly resumes his place on her lap. He is entirely at home with this state of affairs. "Hang on, both of you!" we tell them.

Now everybody's here. Danny gets behind the cart to give it extra momentum to push through the deep sand that's accumulated at the foot of the hill. We roar off to view the garden, where peas and spinach are just poking through; the still-tranquil pond where Victor's trout lurk; the dressage driving ring with its view of our only flat space, a meadow once reserved for brood-mares and their foals; and the woods road lined with hickory trees leading to our biggest and most distant pasture, the one we call The Elysian Field. Luckily, the horses come into view as we arrive and Paul, whose new word this is, speaks for the first time. "Horse!" he says emphatically. Not *horsie*, but *horse*.

Nicole takes it all in with her usual aplomb. "You really *do* live in the woods," she says, but it's hard to tell whether she thinks we're certifiably crazy (the commonly held view) or profoundly blessed to be surrounded by fields and forests and granite ledges. She loved the cart ride, she loved getting to see the horses, and so did her child.

Little Paul is shy at first, surrounded by strangers.

Bacon and orange juice help to bring him into the circle around the table; he and Noah divide the first waffle. Our own maple syrup adds to the mix. Soon, he is tearing off bits of waffle and dipping them in syrup.

Noah is amusing Paul, who is happily pulling the window shades up and down. We linger at the table talking. Nicole says she drives everywhere, she's put seven thousand miles on her car since November.

"Do you still go back to the rehab hospital?"

"Three times a week. Once in the pool, once for real PT, and the third time I just get to work out alone on the machines."

"I'm still working out with the dumbbells," I tell her. "I'm gaining on it. Now, every morning, I spend ten minutes picking up manure in the motel lobby after I put the horses in. It's a funny thing to be proud of. But six weeks ago I could hardly raise the manure fork with two hands."

"You see? I figure my job is to stay as fit as possible. With all the new experiments they're doing on nerve regeneration, I want to be in the front ranks when they come looking for human volunteers."

"They say they're closing in on it. They've had some real success with mice."

"Within ten years," Nicole says. "I'm twenty-one,

I figure that in my lifetime they're going to find a way to spark across these gaps. I mean to be there when that happens. I *know* I'm going to walk again."

I tell her, "I'm planning to stick around for that. I want to be there cheering."

Just before she leaves, Nicole tells me she's been offered a part-time job in the office of a company that leases recreational vehicles to the handicapped. She figures it will be a good stopgap until August, when she enrolls in her first graduate course in social work at Boston College. I lean in the front seat of the car to give her a farewell hug.

"Next time at my place," she says. "And let's try to get Richard and Ann down, too."

April 23

Most afternoons when I climb the hill to pace my mile around the ring, I try to time my walk to coincide with Victor working Boomer under saddle, or my former carriage-driving navigator riding Deuter. I envy their easy posture as they flow past me trotting, looping in large circles, then picking up a canter. I'm torn between such jealousy that I almost wish I weren't here to watch and the deep pleasure I take in seeing my horses in action.

For weeks now I've been thinking about getting up on my horse. I don't have any big plans to ride him, but I have this dogged faith that just walking around while another person leads Deuter will help me reestablish my balance. After all, we're financial supporters of a local riding-for-the-handicapped program; we even donated an aging bombproof pony mare who could tolerate the lifting and positioning of a young patient on her broad back. Why not our own therapeutic riding program?

Today the three of us enter into a conspiracy: with their steadying hands and the help of the mounting block I normally use to climb over my garden fence, I am going to sit on my horse.

Deuter stands like a rock while I shakily attempt to mount. It is very hard to get my right leg over his side; he waits while I take a handful of mane and, with Victor steadying me, haul myself into position. I look around me. I've been planning this for so long! I thought regaining my seat in the saddle would bring with it some sort of epiphany, a revelation of huge consequence. Instead, I feel merely at home. I am back in my peaceful kingdom.

From this new perspective, the crowns of the maples are just beginning to redden. One final pocket of snow along the brook catches the afternoon sun. The raucous calls of pileated woodpeckers sound from the shagbark hickories. They're getting ready to nest. The whole impetuous natural world is poised to burst forth. We begin our stately procession, Deuter obediently following Victor.

I close my eyes, let my hips absorb my horse's familiar cadence, let my torso follow the motion. I am letting myself believe I will heal.